knit 1 bike 1

69 days, 21 workshops and some yarn...

Janet Renouf-Miller

Published in May 2016 by

Lowimpact.org

lili@lowimpact.org
www.lowimpact.org

Copyright © 2016 Janet Renouf-Miller

ISBN 978-0-9954702-0-0

Picture acknowledgements
All photographs by Janet and Lee Renouf-Miller

Printed in Great Britain by
Lightning Source, Milton Keynes

contents

illustrations..5

about the author...10

introduction..11

the trip...21

day 1, 29th June: Dalmellington to Ayr....................................21

day 2, 30th June: Doonfoot, Ayr to the Island of Arran...............26

day 3, 1st July: the first 'solo' day...29

day 4, 2nd July: Kildonan to Lochranza, Isle of Arran................31

day 5, 3rd July: Lochranza to Tarbert, Argyll & Bute..................35

day 6, 4th July: Tarbert to Lochgilphead...................................39

day 7, 5th July: Quaker meeting in Tarbert................................41

day 8, 6th July: Lochgilphead to Kilmartin................................44

day 9, 7th July: something may have changed forever...............45

day 10, 8th July: the Island of Mull, Craignure to Tobermory.........46

day 11, 9th July: Tobermory to Oban..53

day 12, 10th July: from the campsite to Oban & back................56

day 13, 11th July: Oban to Fort William....................................58

day 14, 12th July: a pyjama day..60

day 15, 13th July: an artistic visit...61

day 16, 14th July: Mallaig Craft Group.....................................62

day 17, 15th July: train to Glenfinnan, cycle to Fort William.........64

day 18 16th July – Fort William to Dalmally..............................67

day 19, 17th July: crocheted flowers at Dalmally......................70

day 20, 18th July: Skye beckons...71

day 21, 19th July: Armadale to Ashaig via Broadford.................74

day 22, 20th July: Ashaig to Broadford and back.......................77

day 23, 21st July: Broadford to Plockton..................................79

day 24, 22nd July: in and out of Plockton.................................80

day 25, 23rd July: a real day off – well almost... 82

day 26, 24th July: Dingwall...84

day 27, 25th July: a day in Dingwall...87

day 28, 26th July: Dingwall to Inverness...................................90

day 29, 27th July: Inverness to Aviemore by train......................92

day 30, 28th July: Rothiemurchus to Aviemore & back...............93

day 31, 29th July: Rothiemurchus to Newtonmore......................96

day 32, 30th July: Newtonmore to Blair Atholl...........................98

day 33, 31st July: Blair Atholl to Dunkeld and getting lost...........101

day 34, 1st Aug: getting things sorted out.................................103

day 35, 2nd Aug: the Birnam Institute......................................105

day 36, 3rd Aug: Dunkeld to Dundee....................................107
day 37, 4th August: Dundee to Newburgh...........................110
day 38, 5th August: Newburgh to Kinross...........................112
day 39, 6th Aug: cycled 4 miles...114
day 40, 7th August: Kinross to Stirling................................115
days 41 & 42, 9th/10th August: Stirling to Paisley...........117
day 43, 10th August: Paisley to Lanark and Kirkfieldbank............119
day 44, 11th August: New Lanark World Heritage Site...............120
day 45, 12th August: Kirkfieldbank to Biggar....................124
day 46, 13th August: cycled half a mile.............................127
day 47, 14th August: Cycled half a mile.............................128
day 48, 15th August: Broughton Spinners' Gathering...............128
day 49, 16th August: Biggar to Edinburgh.........................130
day 50, 17th August: the Edinburgh Festival......................131
day 51, 18th August. Colinton to Penicuik..........................135
day 52, 19th August: Penicuik to Longniddry.....................137
day 53, 20th August, workshop..142
day 54, 21st August: Longniddry to Innerwick...................143
day 55, 22nd August: two weeks to go...............................145
day 56, 23rd August: Innerwick to St Abbs.........................146
day 57, 24th August: a day off..148
day 58, 25th August: St Abbs to Duns................................149
day 59, 26th August: Duns to Kelso....................................151
day 60, 27th August: Kelso to Hawick................................152
day 61, 28th August: into Hawick and back.......................153
day 62, 29th August: a week to go......................................154
day 63, 30st August: Hawick to Langholm..........................155
day 64, 31st August: into Langholm and back....................157
day 65, 1st September: Langholm to Kirtlebridge...............158
day 66, 2nd September: Kirtlebridge to Barnsoul..............160
day 67, 3rd September: Barnsoul to Castle Douglas............163
day 68, 4th September: Castle Douglas to Hawkrigg.............. 165
day 69, 5th September: home at last....................................168
a bit more about the Knit 1 Bike 1 art work........................171
knitted bluebells, harebells, & dandelions – patterns...............173
harebells...174
bluebells...176
crocheted dandelions...176
knitted dandelions..176
other lowimpact.org titles..178
notes..181

illustrations

Map of the trip..9
Fig. 1: changing the bike tyres....................................13
Fig. 2: trying to pack - two days to go.....................17
Fig. 3: the clothes taken on the trip.........................19
Fig. 4: all packed up..21
Fig. 5: neighbours and the Knit n' Natter group see us off.............22
Fig. 6: off we go - Janet and Justine set off.............23
Fig. 7: meeting a penny farthing at Patna.................24
Fig. 8: a first workshop at the Robert Burns Heritage Museum.......25
Fig. 9: Bronwen interviews Justine for the Janet Forsyth show........26
Fig. 10: boarding the Ardrossan to Arran ferry...................28
Fig. 11: the crocheted ferry...28
Fig. 12: the Arran cheese factory...............................32
Fig. 13: Royal Bank of Scotland mobile bank at Kilmory.................33
Fig. 14: the mobile library at Blackwaterfoot.............34
Fig. 15: view from the top on the way to Kilmory.....................35
Fig. 16: a leaky tent at Lochranza..............................35
Fig. 17: Lochranza to Claonaig ferry..........................37
Fig. 18: adapting the rear luggage with a piece of polystyrene.......38
Fig. 19: camera pouch made with double knitting.........................39
Fig. 20: a caricature at Tarbert...................................40
Fig. 21: Ele and Jim at the Empire Travel Lodge.............42
Fig. 22: the crocheted tree...43
Fig. 23: the workshop at Kilmartin.............................45
Fig. 24: road signs on Mull were a bit different.................47
Fig. 25: the bus from Tobermory.................................48
Fig. 26: fish & chips with a Les Routiers award.............49
Fig. 27: the colourful buildings in Tobermory.................49
Fig. 28: the Whale and Dolphin Trust, Tobermory.................50
Fig. 29: the workshop at An Tobar Arts Centre.................51
Fig. 30: on the road from Tobermory to Loch Don.................54
Fig. 31: the workshop at Loch Don..............................56
Fig. 32: Christine at Oban...57
Fig. 33: you are going where with that?.....................58
Fig. 34: the tent drying on Morag's kitchen table.................59
Fig. 35: Morag at her house at Lochailort....................60
Fig. 36: Alison Durbin at Wildwood............................61
Fig. 37: crocheted shells on the beach........................62
Fig. 38: the chip shop in the wall, Mallaig.....................63

Fig. 39: Ginger Knitting Studio, Mallaig................................63
Fig. 40: Mallaig knitting group...64
Fig. 41: the crocheted cake on its plate.............................65
Fig. 42: the steam train at Glenfinnan...............................65
Fig. 43: the new rear rucksack at Fort William....................66
Fig. 44: the crocheted limpets on a rock............................68
Fig. 45: crocheted Glenfinnan Viaduct in progress.............68
Fig. 46: Liz, Sandra and Graham at Dalmally......................69
Fig. 47: the workshop at Dalmally....................................70
Fig. 47a: a lamb visits the workshop at Dalmally................71
Fig. 48: the Help for Heroes walker at Broadford...............75
Fig. 49: the Knit 1 Bike 1 sign at Broadford.......................76
Fig. 50: campsite full at Ashaig near Broadford.................77
Fig. 51: the Handspinner Having Fun at Broadford.............78
Fig. 52: the Plockton weather report.................................80
Fig. 53: Calum on the Sula Mhor.......................................81
Fig. 54: Plockton seals..82
Fig. 55: Joan and Iain at Driseach bed & breakfast............83
Fig. 56: Plockton post office..83
Fig. 57: Chinese cyclist on the train to Inverness...............85
Fig. 58: the folded Brompton in the tent at Dingwall..........86
Fig. 59: knitted worms and other creatures.......................87
Fig. 60: the tandem trike with Aiden.................................88
Fig. 61: the Audax sets off..89
Fig. 62: Denise and Steve, Audax organisers......................90
Fig. 63: the Rollende Camping Hotel at Inverness...............92
Fig. 64: the Active Cafaidh, Aviemore...............................94
Fig. 65: a hedgehog knitted by a Aviemore Knitting Group...94
Fig. 66: Newtonmore, location of the Kaye Adams Show......96
Fig. 67: teacher demonstrates the belt at the Folk Museum...97
Fig. 68: the church at the Folk Museum.............................98
Fig. 69: a trucker's breakfast..99
Fig. 70: the top of Drumochter Pass.................................99
Fig. 71: a Sustrans bench made out of skis.......................100
Fig. 72: Highland cattle at Blair Atholl.............................101
Fig. 73: Dunkeld, which way?...102
Fig. 74: Janet and Lee rendevouz at Dunkeld...................103
Fig. 75: Desperate Dan..104
Fig. 76: penguin sculptures looking smart........................105
Fig. 77: the Birnam Institute..106
Fig. 78: Margaret learns to do stranded knitting...............106
Fig. 79: Knit 1 Bike 1 artwork...107
Fig. 80: Ben from Coupar Angus Cylcing Hub....................108

Fig. 81: the tricycle covered in knitting..*109*
Fig. 82: Leona's washing dries on the pulley system.....................*109*
Fig. 83: the talk at Fluph Yarn shop...*110*
Fig. 84: the Tay Bridge...*111*
Fig. 85: Laura at Little Twist Felt Studio.......................................*112*
Fig. 86: Abernethy Tower...*113*
Fig. 87: neck joug, Abernethy Tower..*114*
Fig. 88: Morag and her sister at Skeins & Bobbins........................*115*
Fig. 89: cakes at Powfoot Milk Bar..*116*
Fig. 90: 'Beat That' women's samba band....................................*117*
Fig. 91: Roxie and Conor at the Old Mill Waterfalls......................*119*
Fig. 92: the Wallace Cave pub...*121*
Fig. 93: Strands Knitting Shop, Lanark...*122*
Fig. 94: New Lanark Heritage Centre...*123*
Fig. 95: Christine in the Yarn Shop at New Lanark........................*123*
Fig. 96: Lanarkshire's red roads are now mostly gone...................*126*
Fig. 97: drying things out at Biggar..*127*
Fig. 98: the Spinners' Gathering at Broughton...............................*129*
Fig. 99: Scottish Fibres at Broughton...*130*
Fig. 100: Star Wars characters...*132*
Fig. 101: the Royal Mile...*132*
Fig. 102: Edinburgh Quaker Meeting House venue.......................*133*
Fig. 103: Pins & Needles knitting shop...*134*
Fig. 104: the workshop at Victoria's...*134*
Fig. 105: a notice at Rosslyn..*135*
Fig. 106: Di and Ken at Penicuik..*136*
Fig. 107: the talk at Penicuik Arts Centre.....................................*136*
Fig. 108: the Preston Grange curator...*139*
Fig. 109: old crane at Preston Grange..*140*
Fig. 110: an old boiler at Preston Grange.....................................*140*
Fig. 111: Prestonpans - I had now gone from coast to coast.........*141*
Fig. 112: Angela, Bill and Kai and Longniddry..............................*141*
Fig. 113: Debbie with her giant sock..*142*
Fig. 114: Haddington spinners - a lively bunch..............................*143*
Fig. 115: giant puffballs on the way to Innerwick..........................*144*
Fig. 116: Jenni, Richard, Finn and Morven....................................*145*
Fig. 117: the workshop at Innerwick...*146*
Fig. 118: the results of the 'yarn pooling' workshop......................*146*
Fig. 119: St. Abbs - Louise in her conservatory............................*147*
Fig. 120: saying goodbye to Louise..*149*
Fig. 121: alpaca drying at the Border Mill.....................................*150*
Fig. 122: the mill's hand-dyed yarns and fibres............................*150*
Fig. 123: the Textile Tower House, Hawick....................................*153*

Fig. 124: a knitted mural in the Borders Textile Tower House.......154
Fig. 125: art work in the cafe opposite the Tower House..............154
Fig. 126: clogs at the campsite in Hawick.....................................155
Fig. 127: welcome to Dumfries & Galloway....................................156
Fig. 128: with the caravan at Langholm..157
Fig. 129: Laura and her daughter at Blue Moon in Langholm.......158
Fig. 130: the Kirtle at Eaglesfield..160
Fig. 131: Fiona with one of her dogs...161
Fig. 132: the Brow Well visited by Robert Burns...........................162
Fig. 133: parrot rescue, Dumfries...162
Fig. 134: an impromptu workshop in the caravan..........................163
Fig. 135: cleaning the bike at Barnsoul..164
Fig. 136: arriving at Hawkrigg caravan site...................................166
Fig. 137: Knit 1 Bike 1 cup cakes..167
Fig. 138: a welcome home party at Hawkrigg................................167
Fig. 139: Bekah and Reuben with the goats at Carsphairn...........168
Fig. 140: Dalmellington at last..169
Fig. 141: Janet gets home...170
Fig. 142: pack of smoked salmon found at the side of the road...171
Fig. 143: sheep's head with brown eyes..172
Fig. 144: crocheted caterpillar..172
Fig. 145: spiders are favourite because they're fellow spinners...173
Fig. 146: Glenfinnan Viaduct, Feb 2016...173
Fig. 147: crocheted and knitted dandelions and bluebells............174

about the author

As a keen cyclist, writer and knitter, Knit 1 Bike 1 has been Janet's dream project. She lives in Ayrshire, Scotland with her husband Lee. Not only is there wonderful cycling in the area, but there is also a strong textile history. Janet's home village of Dalmellington was once a weaving town and is surrounded by quiet country roads and wonderful scenery.

Janet has earned her living as a textile artist and writer for many years. She teaches spinning, weaving and knitting to guilds, voluntary groups and schools, through her company Create With Fibre. Knit 1 Bike 1 is a new departure and arose from Janet's desire to combine textile-based art work with cycling. In addition to this book, Janet created an exhibition from the knitted and crocheted art work that was produced on the Knit 1 Bike 1 journey. Further details of this are available on the Create With Fibre website at www.createwithfibre.co.uk.

Janet loves the idea of slow, low-impact journeys and adventures without the need to get on a plane. She and her husband Lee use cars as little as possible, grow much of their own food, have solar panels at their home and a wood burning stove which is run on foraged and waste wood.

Lowimpact.org also publishes Janet's previous book "How to Spin Just About Anything". It was enthusiastically welcomed by spinners and weavers as one of those rare books that actually does tell you how to spin, with enough detail for people to understand the process.

introduction

getting ready; why am I doing this? help!

It is amazing how even a little bit of extra weight around the hips makes it so much harder to get out of the door and get on the bike. It was the menopause and those damn crisps that did it!

As a result, when preparations for this project began, I was just a bit wider than before and needed to do something about it. Well that didn't work as you will find out, but I did get a whole lot fitter and have a really good time. Aged 57, I felt like an old frump on a bike at times but hey, it's better than sitting at *home* feeling like an old frump.

I basically did it to prove that I can be a tiny bit brave. My dear old Dad was still on his bike and in his hiking boots at 82, just weeks before he died, and that does make it hard to find excuses. It was partly in memory of him that I set myself the challenge of living life to the full, just like he did, and set off to cycle my way around Scotland, knitting and crocheting what I saw on the way.

I crocheted anything, from a strawberry sponge cake to the Glenfinnan Viaduct. Twenty-one free mini workshops took place en route, partly as a way of meeting people and partly to say thank you to those who offered me a bed for the night or a free meal.

As I enjoy doing things with a purpose and also work as a full-time textile artist, this trip seemed an ideal way to combine cycling with all things woolly. It was a good excuse and far more fun than just cycling round Scotland for the sake of it.

The journey was done on a thirteen-year-old Brompton folding bicycle. The Brompton is one of the most compact folding bikes in the world - easily taken on a bus, but still suitable for long rides. Because these bikes are so well made, a thirteen-year-old model is still virtually as good as a brand new one.

The route was very much a meander and not an attempt to absolutely cover the whole country. I cycled where people wanted me to go and did go around a good bit of the country, but I missed out

Grampian because it was just a step too far. The people of Grampian were enthusiastic and it *was* a shame...maybe next time?

It was a lot of fun setting up the workshops via Facebook, and I was a real whizz at social networking by D-Day. Although some of the workshops were for familiar groups, shops and textile artists, some were for new social media friends.

The whole itinerary was in place, including the twenty planned workshops (number twenty-one was a spur of the moment thing), before I set off and I pretty much stuck to the schedule. It was great not having to figure out routes whilst sitting in a tent in the rain, and there was so much else to do, such as crocheting and writing the book.

getting funding

The original idea had been to apply for artistic funding for the project. Ten weeks is a long time to go without an income, and the cost of the trip itself and all the yarn was substantial. However, despite initial interest, references and all kinds of evidence, Creative Scotland pronounced me lacking in the correct experience because I had not done anything similar before. So I set out to prove them wrong, of course.

The Authors' Foundation also said 'no' and time was running out. My crowd funding appeal attracted a good bit of interest but did not reach its all-or-nothing target, which yet again meant no money. The lesson here was that you really need to know what you are doing to succeed with crowd funding.

Finally, I did it my way and simply put a PayPal button on the website and blog. Through that and Facebook, enough was raised to enable the project to happen, although the bulk of it was self-financed. The greatest support came from friends and family, fellow textile artists and business people, with some companies donating yarn and supplies. And of course there were all of those who offered free accommodation or a hot meal en route. Thanks folks, you know who you are.

getting into training

Getting fit for the journey started in October the year before, which *should* have been plenty of time. But I was not fit and had been ignoring minor ailments, so now needed to sort all of that out. A painful knee, caused by hiking up steep cliff-side steps was the first setback, until I finally visited a physiotherapist, who said it was muscle strain and that cycling was good for it. No excuse there then.

Fig. 1: changing the bike tyres

I was back on the bike in earnest until December, when the flu struck. This was followed by a three-week-long chesty cough and although I kept on with the cycling, I could only do shorter distances. The cough was followed in April by sinusitis that just would not go away and I was getting a bit panicky. Why all those ailments *this* year, for goodness sake?

The sinusitis was still bad in early May whilst I was demonstrating at my Spinning and Weaving Guild's exhibition in Dumfries. Fortunately, a fellow spinner who was probably fed up with hearing me sniffing, said her doctor had suggested Ibuprofen, because it was anti-inflammatory. It worked, and within a couple of days all symptoms were gone (thanks Margaret). I am not a medical expert though, so do ask your own doctor!

The best advice came from the official Knit 1 Bike 1 backup team, my husband Lee, who heard it goodness knows where. 'Do not ignore things and deal with any niggles or minor problems smartly.' This rang in my ears throughout the journey and the bike and I both made it home with no injuries or ailments.

After all this, there were a couple of months left to get really fit and it was a case of getting on the bike most days and doing something, even just a few miles. Remarkably, I set off 100% healthy and in reasonably good shape.

By mid June I could cycle twenty miles but was done-for by the end of it. With a fortnight till D-Day, I was due to go to the Lake District in the North of England for a few days on a spinning and weaving retreat. This was an annual event with fellow members of the Dumfries and Galloway Guild of Weavers, Spinners & Dyers (you will hear quite a bit about them in this book) and not wanting to miss it, the bike went with me. Whilst the others spun yarn, I spun the wheels, doing thirty miles for the first time.

I slogged up hills, jumped on ferries and visited Greystokes Cycle Cafe, where you only get to eat if you arrive by bike or on foot. The terrain was hilly and the cycling strenuous. Finally I was confident of making it round Scotland, although being constantly overtaken by speedy locals on road bikes was a tad humbling. (I just *have* to get off to look at things and I tend to average about seven miles an hour.) By watching what these road cyclists did on the roller coaster hills and dips of the Lakeland roads, I learned to free-wheel down hills and then cycle like the clappers up the subsequent rise. It was strenuous but saved a lot of energy.

Two weeks later when setting off for real, I had never carried all of the luggage before, but I could cycle thirty miles in a day, had cycled up plenty of hills and had done an overnight trial camp. It was chilly at night during the trial camp in May, but the departure date would be the end of June and it was bound to be warmer by then. Or so I thought.

the unexpected

A couple of weeks before the trip, the new Schwalbe Marathon Plus tyres had arrived. Hubby and I spent ages trying to get them on the 16 inch Brompton wheels and finally phoned Dales Cycles, the Brompton experts in Glasgow, where the mechanic told me it was easy. 'Just keep pushing the rim of the tyre to the centre of the wheel rim as you do it.'

I came off the phone and impressed Lee by doing it with no bother, using just one tyre lever. BUT...that was when we discovered that the alloy rim on the back wheel was knackered. It had almost worn through with thirteen years of use and needed to be replaced!

Why had I not thought to check the bike ahead of time? Having no experience of doing a longer journey, it was only once it was nearly time to go that I even thought to get new tyres. I was just going to set off without really giving the bicycle a second thought. It was running fine and I had oiled the chain regularly and looked after the brakes after all. It sounds stupid now, but the Brompton had never given any trouble and was so reliable.

the final countdown

14 days to go...Discovered the need for a new back wheel, which includes the hub gears on the Brompton.

13 days...Dental problems. Two fillings dropped out. Both needed crowns but there was no time. They were patched up by an emergency dentist with no guarantee that they would last the 69 days until I returned home. One of them did and one did not, but I managed without it.

12 days...Off to the Physio for a final check up – all in order there at least.

11 days...The bike went in for a new back wheel to be fitted and new bearings on the front. The back wheel on the Brompton includes the hub gears. The fittings had changed since I bought the bike, so it was not a simple job. Thankfully the cycle shop had a wheel in stock.

10 days...The new back wheel sounded like a train when the bike was in 3rd gear...Aaarrgh! lots of time on the phone to Dales Cycles.

9 days...Stiff knees. The new Sturmey Archer gearing was different to that of the old, SRAM hub. It made me cycle harder and faster but also persist in too high a gear thinking "I *can't* need to change gear, I never did before on this hill." Lee took the bike back to Dales Cycles who confirmed it was supposed to sound like a train, but might quieten down a bit with use. It never did, but it got me round Scotland with no problems and eventually I stopped noticing it.

8 days...Radio Scotland decided not to accompany me on part of the journey – oh well.

7 days...The local newspaper, The Ayrshire Post, said they would come to see me off – hurrah! Meanwhile we weighed the tent and discovered it did not weigh 1.2kg but 3kg. How could I not know that? New tent ordered by overnight courier.

6 days... The knees were now behaving and I was getting used to the noise from the new gears on the bike. The tent arrived, a Terra Nova Laser Photon 2 which was a silly price and supposedly weighed 700g. The pegs were bits of titanium wire and would not stay in the ground even in the back garden with no wind. We replaced them with the alloy pegs from the old tent and added a bit of groundsheet to protect the tent floor. It now weighed 1.2kg. That was still a lot lighter than the old one, although I was a bit nervous because the fabric was so thin.

5 days... Radio Scotland phoned. The Janice Forsyth Show wanted to interview me at the workshop on Day 1. Fingers crossed this time.

4 Days... Lowimpact.org – who would be publishing the book – confirmed that it could be printed in full colour. A big relief, as textile photos in black and white are a bit underwhelming.

3 days... The route planning was finished. Well, more like I gave up on it. After Lanark on the way home, there would be no cities to find my way into and out of and I would be in familiar territory. It turned out that the CTC route planner was impossible to follow anyway, because it is not obvious, to me at least, which village or town you are in when you emerge from a cycle track onto a road. The road map worked better. I had stiff knees again and had *put on* weight! Having resolved to lighten the load by losing a couple of kilos, I had done the opposite! How could this be, with all that cycling? It must be muscle.

2 days... It won't all fit in the bags! The pile of stuff I intended to take had spent the last week as a centrepiece in the living room. It had been trimmed down drastically and still would not fit. I only had a wee cycle today, but all uphill, and the knees were much better.

1 day... Facebook, the blog and website were up to date. The itinerary and 20 mini workshops were all organised and the newsletter had gone. Justine, my cycle partner for the first two days, cycled over on her bike, to deliver it in readiness for the following day.

I had a lovely time over soup with her and her dad George, then some more friends called Lucy and Andrew showed up. Neighbours Stephen and wee Jack delivered rhubarb cake and the front garden had been yarn bombed and decorated with bunting. Quite a party – and now I just needed to pack those bags...

deciding what to take

It was easy deciding what to take and I had some really good ideas. The hard part was deciding what *not* to take, given that a large trailer was not part of the plan. Somehow knitting needles, crochet hooks and yarn had to fit into the bike bag along with 70 days' worth of spare knickers and the camping equipment.

The first step had been to lay it all out in a giant heap and brutally prune. What was left was a pile that still included the same quantity of yarn and knitting needles but only two pairs of knickers. In other words I took the same amount of 'essentials' as you would for a weekend trip.

Fig. 2: trying to pack - two days to go

what I did not take

So here is the list of what I reluctantly rejected... and I never missed it one bit.

- Camping stove
- Plate, mug, ultra-light pots and pans
- All the books I wanted to read
- Ordnance Survey maps for the whole of Scotland

- Print outs of the whole route from the CTC route planner
- Spare clothes

what I did take, in addition to what I was wearing

- Tent, sleeping bag, sheet liner, self-inflating mat
- Water bottle
- Dry emergency food such as oatcakes, plus enough additional food for the day
- Too much yarn, wound into small balls in many colours
- Four crochet hooks, three sets of small double-pointed knitting needles and two circular knitting needles
- Spectacles
- Phone, extra battery and charger. I bought a new phone with a larger screen, choosing the cheapest one. That turned out to be a mistake, but more about that later
- Two fold out maps of Scotland, with the excess parts removed
- Sewing kit
- Small, jotter-style notebook and pens
- First aid kit containing plasters, micropore tape, Steri-Strips, a bandage, sterile dressings, comfrey ointment, tweezers, tick twizzler
- Tiny plastic bottles/pots of TCP, sun tan lotion, heat lotion and moisturiser, bicarbonate of soda deodorant
- A sliver of soap and another of shampoo bar, a one-inch strip of flannel for washing myself and an actual flannel to use as a towel
- Folding hairbrush
- Toothbrush, dental floss, toothpaste, plus an assortment of inter-dental brushes to deal with the gaps caused by those missing fillings.
- One spare set of underwear and socks, two tee shirts (used for sleeping in too), a fleece top, merino undershirt, long johns, a pair of lightweight trousers and a hanky. (Tissues are no good when wet so a hanky is a good cycling accessory.)
- Pair of sandals

- Sudocrem and Vaseline in small pots (essential long distance cycling equipment)
- Tiny LED bike light which was also good for use in the tent
- Tool kit containing tyre levers, spanners, a multi tool allen key thing, rags, a tiny bottle of oil and a puncture repair kit
- Two spare inner tubes
- Bicycle helmet, cycling glasses, waterproof jacket and trousers and, of course, the bike

Fig. 3: the clothes taken on the trip

getting it all on the bike

The day before setting off, all this stuff was *still* just a pile in the living room. The main luggage on the Brompton is carried on the front of the bike, which is unusual. There is a large clip on the front of the frame and the bag just slots onto it. Because the bag is on the frame and not on the wheel or handlebars, you hardly notice it when cycling. In fact, the bike feels weird without the luggage, because you get so used to it being there.

For the purposes of this trip, it was necessary to take rear luggage as well. I was blasé about this, having taken a rear pannier on a short trip before by strapping it to the underneath of the seat, like you would a saddle bag. I had a great bag, bought cheaply years before, which also had straps to convert it into a rucksack. Ideal, I thought, and I was glad of an excuse to use it again at last.

This old bag was the subject of some heated discussion in our household, as Lee maintained that it was too old to survive the journey and that I needed something 'proper'. We looked everywhere and finally bought a seat-post rack to go on the bike. Lee had an alternative rucksack and the combination of the two should work. After that I somehow managed to forget about it, finally trying it all out just a couple of days before setting off.

The rack was not a success. Even attached at the lowest point on the seat post, the distance between it and the seat itself was too short to accommodate the rucksack. We tried all sorts of permutations with bits of rope and straps, lashed the bag on sideways and packed the bags themselves in different ways, but none of it worked. The rear bag would just swing around when I was cycling and get in the way. We tried a second, smaller Brompton bag suspended from the saddle. This worked but was not large enough to accommodate the tent and sleeping mat. Lee even made up a gadget for the rear bag to rest on, but nothing did the job.

So I set off minus the seat post rack and with the old rear pannier. I clipped it to the seat, added a cover, then lashed it in place with a bit of orange nylon rope. It caught on my heels a bit if the angle was not just right, needed frequent repairs (yes, you were right, Lee) and was a blooming nuisance, until it was finally replaced by a new rucksack in Fort William.

the trip

day 1, Monday 29th June: Dalmellington, East Ayrshire to Ayr, South Ayrshire, 15 miles

What a send off! After a restless night thinking about how to fit everything into the bag and a final emergency pruning and re-pack at 6.30am, I was ready. Yes, it really was 6.30 am on the day of departure before the packing issue was more or less resolved! The rear bag was still problematic but more or less worked and I set off saying that if it got me to Oban (day eight), it could be sorted out then. Oh heck – what had I done? After a year of planning, the whole project felt rather unreal, which was probably just as well.

Fig. 4: all packed up

The weight of the bike plus bags was at least manageable after that final prune, although still rather heavy and it was a bit of a job to get the bike down the front steps. (Because my Brompton is a folding bike, it lives in the hall beside Lee's red one rather than in the garage.) I was to reduce the contents of the bags further as the journey progressed but at this stage everything seemed essential. How could it possibly weigh so much?

Yarn was important but at the last minute was reduced to two bags instead of three. Every square inch of the cycle bags was packed solid and letting go of some yarn did save bulk even if it did not weigh much. Eventually, I learned that you can only work on one thing at a time and kept a list of things to knit or crochet, so two or three balls of yarn was enough. At the start though I had little idea *what* I would be creating let alone what yarn it would require.

Justine would be my cycle partner for the first two days. As the principal art teacher at the local high school, she had commissioned me to do weaving and knitting workshops there with the students in the months before setting off. We got talking and one thing led to another. The pupils were following Justine's progress as she cycled with me and she had put information about Knit 1 Bike 1 on the school blog.

Justine arrived at 9.30 just in time to hear me wondering whether I should unpack the bags again. Fortunately I did not, because the Local paper arrived at 9.45 for a photocall. The Dalmellington Knit 'n' Blether group (the bunting and yarn bombing in the front garden was down to them) and some of the neighbours turned up to see me off, and we left on schedule at 10.00.

It was to be quite a full-on first day, with a press interview then a fifteen mile ride to Ayr on the west coast of Scotland, followed by a workshop at the Robert Burns Birthplace Museum. The Janice Forsyth Show from Radio Scotland were coming along to the workshop to interview everyone which added to the pressure just a bit. I set off thinking 'This is not really happening.'

Fig. 5: neighbours and the Knit n' Natter group see us off - L-R: Marion, Ella, Lyn, Jenny, Lyssa and Jack

Fig. 6: off we go - Janet and Justine set off

It was a brisk 15 mile cycle to Ayr – well, brisk for me, on a loaded Brompton folding bicycle. Justine, a sprightly 30-something cruised along on her super lightweight road bike. She was going home overnight so had no luggage to carry. Every time I looked in the rear view mirror she did not seem to be pedalling. Cycling for the first time whilst fully laden, I pushed myself to go a bit faster than was quite comfortable, not wanting Justine to get too bored. And yes, my ego may have had just a little bit to do with it.

I had done the trial cycle and camp at a local campsite, owned by friends Jane and Andrew, and carried the tent, sleeping mat and sleeping bag on the bike no bother. I knew a few clothes and some yarn would add a bit of weight but not much.

The additional weight was considerably more than expected though, what with extra food, yarn, clothes, spare inner tubes, a first aid kit and the precious sandals which I insanely took even though they weighed 500g. I had the idea that being July, the weather would be hot and wanted to be able to change from hiking boots into something cooler after a hard day's cycling. The sandals eventually went home and were not missed due to the almost total lack of warm evenings.

Justine was kind and suggested lots of breaks which I am sure she did not need as much as I did. We got as far as Patna, the next village along the road and stopped in amazement when a guy on a penny farthing came the other way. He was cycling from John

O'Groats to Lands End to raise money for a 'cycling without age' project (www.rideoncycling.org).

His bike had solid tyres and the rear one had split. He was hoping to get to Carlisle in the north of England before it fell to bits. Whilst we spoke, his bike was propped up against a bus shelter and I guessed that something tall to hang onto probably came in handy when you stopped on a penny farthing.

workshop number 1: The Robert Burns Birthplace Museum, Alloway, Ayrshire

I had originally imagined a low-key affair for the first workshop but was even more delighted when Bronwen Livingstone asked to come along and do a radio interview for the Janice Forsyth Show. Bronwen was lovely and a keen knitter herself, so she fitted in just fine. All of the workshop participants were quite happy to help out by being on the radio.

Fig. 7: meeting a penny farthing at Patna

The workshop was a problem-solving knitting and crochet 'clinic'. Maggie brought along a crocheted elephant with a wobbly head and Sheila a sheep with wonky horns. There were some blankets that were hard to sew up, including one from Doon Academy Art Department's Community Knit Along, courtesy of Justine. And Maureen wanted to make toe up socks and learn to do grafting. Chris, the Learning Manager from the Museum had organised everything for us and made sure we had lots of the Museum's delicious hand-made shortbread.

a bed for the night

Lyn, a good friend from my local spinning group, Ayrshire Handspinners and Weavers, had offered overnight accommodation in Ayr. I spent a nice evening with Lyn, husband Stuart and Max the Labradoodle. Max and I played ball, then he settled down on top of my foot, making me feel all warm and fuzzy. So there I was, staying with friends half an hour's drive from home and close to where I normally went to buy groceries – a bit surreal.

Fig. 8: a first workshop at the Robert Burns Heritage Museum

I did not get any crocheting or knitting done on that first day but took some good photographs for inspiration and headed to bed feeling that the project had got off to a good start. Justine went home for the night because she lived nearby and we had arranged to meet at Ayr railway station the following day.

It really helped being with friends and I even calmed down a bit. I was to receive a similar welcome throughout the journey and without the many folk who put me up for the night, fed me and hosted workshops it would have been a miserable and lonely affair indeed. A delicious tea of salmon and all the trimmings set me up for the next day's cycling but feeling so excited did not make for a good night's sleep. Must get the recipe for that amazing flax bread, Lyn...

Fig. 9: Bronwen interviews Justine for the Janet Forsyth show

day 2, Tuesday 30th June: Doonfoot, Ayr to the Island of Arran, 21.5 miles

We almost missed the ferry. After a second night tossing and turning with a head full of ideas, I was wide awake at 5am and gave up. The old brain still kept thinking 'I am really doing this, I am really doing this' over and over, waking me with a jolt every time. So crocheting a tree and planning the day a bit seemed like a better use of the time and I got busy. Was there anything in the bags that was not essential? I jettisoned a small ball of aqua yarn, only to wonder if I should keep it. How much yarn and in what colours would be needed before meeting up with Lee in Oban in a week's time - who knew?

The route of choice for cyclists going up the west of Scotland usually involves cycling to Ardrossan on the west coast, catching the ferry to the Island of Arran and cycling over the Island. From Arran, there is a second short hop by ferry from Lochranza to Claonaig and then you are on the Mull of Kintyre, with a nice quiet road all the way to Lochgilphead in Argyll and Bute. There are trains or a cycle way from Glasgow to Ardrossan so it is a handy route even for overseas visitors.

The main alternative route north from Glasgow, the A82 has a cycle path for much of the way but the nine mile busy and narrow Loch Lomond stretch does not. There is a wall on one side and the Loch on the other, blind bends and coaches full of tourists. Not a healthy mix for those of us on two wheels.

So Justine and I met at Ayr station (a civilised one mile cycle from Lyn and Stuart's house) and fortunately we both bought through tickets for the boat and train. We needed to change trains at Kilwinning in order to get the "boat train" to Ardrossan, but being busy talking we missed the stop!

Admittedly this was an unusual train, because it was a super duper express with only one stop instead of the usual half a dozen. Kilwinning was the first stop and the next and final one after that was Glasgow, forty minutes further on.

This was a major crisis because the Sainsbury's Cafe Sock Knitting Group were meeting us on the ferry and I did not have anyone's mobile number. It looked like they would be on the ferry without us. So we panicked, then panicked some more and finally posted on Facebook that we may miss the ferry. Not that any of them were at all likely to be looking at Facebook.

I phoned Lee several times to see if he could buy us the bicycle tickets we needed before boarding, in the hope we might catch the ferry in the nick of time. He did not pick up and I was busy planning to send flowers to entire sock group, when the conductor (train manager) joined in the conversation. She went off muttering 'leave it to me' and returned ten minutes later saying 'we have a plan'.

A train would depart from Glasgow a few minutes after we arrived there and get us to Ardrossan South Beach, 2.5 miles from the ferry terminal. Providing we cycled like the clappers, we would make it. The conductor walked us through the station and onto the next train, where we sat poised for action for a good 15 minutes, until some fellow cyclists suggested that we could, in fact remove our helmets and relax a bit as the journey back down would take the best part of an hour.

Justine took charge in true teacherly fashion when we arrived at Ardrossan South Beach and used the GPS on her iPhone to navigate from one station to the other. We made it in good time and there was Lee on the quayside cheering us on and saying we did not need tickets for the bikes after all.

Caledonian MacBrayne with their familiar black, white and red ferries serve just about every Scottish island and I was to use several of them in the course of the journey. I had even started to crochet the

Isle of Mull ferry before setting off, using polystyrene as a form for the shape.

Fig. 10: boarding the Ardrossan to Arran ferry

Fig. 11: the crocheted ferry

We met up with the sock knitters in the cafe on the boat as planned and they were laid back about the whole nearly-missing-the-ferry thing. We ate heartily – more because of all that nervous energy than anything to do with having cycled a total of 3.5 miles so far. As we had boarded the ferry, one of the Cal-Mac staff pointed out that there was a bit of yarn dangling from my bike. It seemed that all of the yarn and crochet hooks had fallen out from under the waterproof cover on the rear bag, where I had stuffed them in haste.

Tricia from the group loaned me a crochet hook but I was too excited to do anything. When we arrived in Brodick I managed to get some yarn from a charity shop. So much for all that agonising over what yarn to take. It was rather a relief, actually to just have one ball each of grey, green and brown.

First port of call was Brodick Castle gardens where there was a Woolly Woods yarn bombing project. It was a surprisingly long way to the Castle, which is not in the town at all. There were some nice knitted and crocheted flowers but not much else to be seen and we headed off back the way we had come, then on to Kildonan campsite on the south of the island.

The road to Kildonan was like a roller coaster and the steep uphills were followed by demoralising downhill sections, only to go right back up again. Arran was just about the toughest cycle of the whole trip and it was funny how my mind had smoothed those hills out over the years since last I cycled there.

We stopped for a cuppa and lots more food at Lamlash, then toiled onwards. I was envious of Justine's luggage free state. She had decided not to join me in the camping field and booked into the adjacent hotel. Never had a glass of lager with fish and chips tasted so good and oh, the joys of a beach side campsite right next to a hotel with facilities. I was just about wired to the moon with adrenalin and spent another restless night in the unaccustomed new tent. I did not envy Justine her luxury hotel room one bit. No really, I did not – honest - especially when she posted a picture of it on Facebook...

day 3, Wednesday 1st July: the first 'solo' day, 1.5 miles

A goodbye cooked breakfast with Justine at the hotel was well worth the £8.50 it cost. She was headed back home and set off for Brodick the long way round, meaning she would have cycled all the way round the island by the time she caught the ferry. I would be following the same route as far as Lochranza the following day but not of course doing the final eight miles back to Brodick.

After going through the front bag and re-packing, things were a bit more organised and although Justine had been great company I was also looking forward to some time alone in order to settle down a bit. Checking over the new tent, I got to know it a little and managed to pitch it somewhat better. I still did not trust it to withstand really bad weather but hey, this was July after all.

A nap really helped with both the tiredness and the constant state of nervous energy. The bike bag made a reasonable back rest whilst writing and crocheting in the tent and I even did some laundry. The missing yarn turned up whilst re-packing the bags of course and had not fallen out after all.

Bolstered by a mid-afternoon lager and slice of cake, I set off on a steep, one mile cycle up the hill out of the bay to visit Judith, an 82 year-old fellow Quaker and textile artist. She had sent a message inviting me to visit when she heard about the project.

Judith was a fascinating and resourceful person who had support and friendship around her simply because of the kind of person she was. We spent a lovely afternoon chatting and she gave me some yarn from her huge, well catalogued collection, left over from her career in textiles. I chose small amounts of several types that could be used for making seashells. This gave me the idea of collecting small bits of yarn from as many of those I visited as possible and including it in the work produced for the Knit 1 Bike 1 exhibition.

There were hooded crows in Judith's garden. They are only found in the north of Scotland and the islands and I had never seen one before. They were on the Knit 1 Bike 1 bucket list (see below), so that was one thing ticked off. In the evening, I continued to crochet the tree, which should not have taken this long but true to form I was getting distracted by other things.

Even by day three, the trip had involved getting to know people better and meeting new ones, which continued to be one of the most delightful things about it. Being on a bike and having a 'project' led to deeper and more personal discussions, with less need for a formal introduction. It made it easier to meet others who had equally interesting projects of their own without really trying – like the guy on the penny farthing.

Being on a bike is a great way to meet people and folks just seem to stop and chat. Today I learned that a couple on the campsite were planning to go round the world in their Land Rover and it would take them two years. Check out Ruby Landy on Facebook.

I went to sleep thinking:

a) That this trip was going to be easier than I thought. Which just shows how wrong you can be.

b) That I needed a microwavable bowl to make porridge in. This campsite had a microwave and kettle, so presumably quite a few subsequent sites would too. Wrong again.

c) I was proud that, at 57 and after ten years of thinking my back would get too sore to do it, I was really back in the camping groove again. Right this time.

the Knit 1 Bike 1 bucket list

1. See some hooded crows – done
2. Have a slab of Rocky Road, even though it is bad for me – done. I sneaked a huge slab of Rocky Road at the Brodick Castle tearoom and it was awesome.
3. See the 'Woolly Woods' project in Brodick Castle Gardens – done.
4. Become able to sleep anywhere and get a good night's sleep in a different bed each night. A work in progress – more practice needed.
5. Develop greater independence of mind and self-sufficiency skills whilst travelling. Certainly done by the time I got home, mostly by being too tired to think all the time.
6. Be able to navigate around Scotland without getting hopelessly lost. Done – yes, really.

day 4, Thursday 2nd July: Kildonan to Lochranza, Isle of Arran, 30 miles and a reality check...

I slept. Got cosied up in the tent with some crochet the previous night from 8.30pm onwards and by 11pm the main part of the tree was finished, although it still needed more leaves. So at least there would be something to show the folks at workshop number two, in Lochranza the following day. It was tempting to start on some shells with the new yarn from Judith but no, for once I decided to finish what I had started first. Although eventually I learned to accept that doing one thing at a time just slows me down and leads to boredom.

Mine was a different rhythm to the holiday makers around me and what with writing the book, crocheting, blogging and putting updates on Facebook there was hardly a minute to spare. It also took longer to pack up when travelling by bike and the vast majority of folk had come by car.

Having been in one place for a couple of days, it was hard to remember how everything fitted in the bags, which would not close properly. Given it was July and lovely weather I parcelled up the thermals (big mistake), a heavy duty plastic bag, excess yarn and a crochet hook ready to send home. Despite getting up at 6.30am it was 9.30 before I was ready to leave the campsite. Another half an hour was spent stopping and trying to figure out how to secure the rear bag so that it did not bump my heels. It had been OK on days one and two. Then I had to push the bike up the very steep hill out of the bay.

So getting properly underway took until 10am. I did not feel like a 'real' camping cyclist at all and was very glad no one was there to see. The precious Spork (spoon and fork combined) that Lee had given me as a leaving present was nowhere to be seen and never did turn up. Given the subsequent Spork challenges, it became known as Spork no 1.

Fig. 12: the Arran cheese factory

I recalled wrongly that the road to Lochranza was flat and an easy cycle. It only levelled out later on and the first 15 miles were even steeper than the previous section from Brodick to Kildonan. The

Arran Cheese Factory at Kilmory was a much-needed pit stop and I enjoyed a cup of tea and oatcakes whilst watching cheese being made.

There was a mobile bank parked at Kilmory and on a whim I stopped and got money out. Because there was no mobile reception or internet, they asked for ID which I did not have. I must have looked trustworthy because they did a signature check and gave me the money. This was a lucky call, as it was several days before I would have access to a bank again.

The strenuous rollercoaster of a ride continued all the way to Blackwaterfoot but with wonderful scenery from the tops. One of the descents was so steep that there is a warning notice for cyclists. Every year someone tries to freewheel down it and comes to grief on the bend at the bottom.

I celebrated arriving in Blackwaterfoot by buying a wheat free loaf at a craft bakery shop and just could not cram the food in quickly enough. There was a mobile library in Blackwaterfoot and it made me think how much we take things like that for granted. So I took a photo of it and resolved to crochet both the library and the mobile bank. So very Scottish.

Fig. 13: Royal Bank of Scotland mobile bank at Kilmory, Arran

I posted the surplus clothes and yarn home and after more pottering about and doing some writing, it was 2.30pm. Fortunately I squeezed the rest of the bread and some bananas into the bike bag, even though it would not shut properly. Fortunate, because otherwise there would have been no dinner that evening.

The second half of the journey was a flat and easy ride in lovely sunshine. There was no hurry – or so I thought - so I had another stop at the golf club cafe a few miles further on. They offered me a free cup of tea because of the project, although I managed to resist eating any more cake.

Fig. 14: the mobile library at Blackwaterfoot, Arran

On reaching Lochranza, the weather changed and the first drops of rain began to fall. This quickly became a torrential downpour, followed by the worst midges ever encountered. If only I had got there sooner the tent would have been pitched before the rain.

The village shop turned out to be just a gift shop at the local distillery which had closed at 4pm. The actual food shop was in Pirnmill six miles back the way. I was too knackered to attempt another twelve mile round trip on top of the thirty already done, even for food. And the midges were too awful even to risk venturing out to the pub.

Having bought a microwavable container, there was no food to microwave and none of the subsequent campsites *had* a microwave. So after a dinner of bread and bananas, I turned in for the night feeling rather lonely and with no internet or phone reception. The microwavable container stayed in the bag until Lanark for some reason and then I finally dumped it.

It rained heavily throughout the night and midges congregated between the fly sheet and inner tent, turning the fabric black. A foray to the loos meant spending 10 minutes killing hundreds of them with a towel after they got into the tent. I did try to do some crocheting but ended up spending most of the time killing midges. That and doing a dance to get enough of a phone signal to send Lee a text, letting him know I had arrived safely.

Fig. 15: view from the top on the way to Kilmory

day 5, Friday 3rd July: Lochranza to Tarbert, Argyll & Bute, 13 miles

The state of the art £345 tent leaked after a night of heavy rain and the inner tent was covered in water droplets. Most had fortunately not come inside but some had. Things were damp but there were no actual puddles. So no more camping until the tent had been proofed, given the forecast for the west coast and the islands was now rain, rain and more rain.

Fig. 16: a leaky tent at Lochranza

In the morning, the midges were thick round the door of the tent and there was a coating of them between the fly sheet and inner tent. It was impossible to get in or out without being savaged and a midge net was essential. For those who do not know, a midge net is made from fine mesh and encloses the head completely. It is the only thing that works when the midges are really bad and between June and September no self respecting Scot would camp in the West of Scotland without one.

workshop number 2

Down to earth with a bump after two lovely days of sunshine and it had been chilly during the night without the thermals. I had worn all my clothes inside the sleeping bag and was still not warm enough to get a good night's sleep. This was a taste of things to come, as the chilly, wet weather was to continue for most of July.

So I tumbled out of the tent, ravaged by midges after a stormy, damp night and made a frugal breakfast of the remaining bread and by now very squashed bananas.

The Day's project was a spinning and knitting workshop for The Arran Guild of Weavers, Spinners & Dyers at the house of one of the members. It was a couple of miles to Pam's house on the other side of the bay and hopefully I arrived looking like nothing was amiss. She declared the previous evening's midges the worst she had ever seen. They had actually been coming in under her back door, which was unheard of. Pam had provided some gluten free cakes and she must have wondered at me cramming them in at *quite* such a rate but I was very hungry after such a scant breakfast and a meagre dinner the night before.

Ruth had brought her spinning wheel and we looked at different ways to spin silk. Pam had a problem doing the last 'row' of her entrelac squares. Although these are usually squares joined to look like diamond shapes, the first and last rows are triangles in order to create a straight edge. We also discussed gauge and sampling to get the correct size of garment, how to make a shrug and using handspun yarn in knitting projects.

Then we had a go at double knitting, great fun and really easy. There was an awesome onion tart and salad for lunch and of course lots of chat. Again I ate rather a lot, finishing off seconds and probably depriving Pam's husband of a light snack later. Pam mentioned that the weather was to be stormy the following day and ferries were likely to be cancelled.

I decided to pack up immediately after the workshop rather than endure another night of torrential rain and midges followed by no breakfast. After a lightning pack-up and super-speedy ride, I just made the 3pm tiny Lochranza to Claonaig (pronounced Clonaig) ferry. It was running late which was a stroke of luck. There was a snack bar just by the ferry terminal which was open – it had been shut the day before - and there was enough time to buy some food for the 13 mile cycle on the other side.

A group of men on mountain bikes were waiting alongside a mountain of luggage, topped by a stirrup pump. The luggage was following them by taxi from hotel to hotel and I was agog at how much luggage they had for a just a few days' cycling.

They, on the other hand were well impressed that not only was I carrying enough for 69 days but was camping as well and cycling on a folding bike. They cheered me up and when I took their photograph named themselves the 'Lincoln Lads'. At the other side, they waved and set off earnestly for Tarbert but I got ahead when one of them had a puncture. And the stirrup pump was, of course in the taxi...

Fig. 17: Lochranza to Claonaig ferry with the Lincolnshire Lads

After a few miles of steep hills in glorious sunshine on the other side - a stark contrast to the rain and midges at Lochranza - the road levelled out. The rear luggage was being a nuisance again and looking round for something to keep it away from my heels, I spotted a piece of polystyrene just the right size. Wedging this between the bag and the bike did the trick, thankfully. I stopped at the first hotel, having almost reached Tarbert and got the last room there for a pricey £69.50. The Tarbert seafood festival was on though and I was lucky to get it.

A reasonably priced but delicious meal of scallops, chips and lager at the hotel set me up just fine. And joy of joys the room had a hot bath, linen sheets and squishy pillows. I crocheted one leaf for the tree(!)

but then undid it by mistake in a lager-induced haze whilst sorting through the bag of yarn. Oh well.

Fig. 18: adapting the rear luggage with a piece of polystyrene

The tiny single room was a bit chaotic, what with the tent and sleeping mat spread out to dry and laundry hanging up. I hoped no one would come up to offer me room service. Everything had to be unpacked and re-packed after the hasty departure from Lochranza and there was still no sign of Spork no. 1. The wind got up during the night and it was lovely listening to gales and lashing rain from the comfort of a warm bed. Leaving Arran a day early and booking into the hotel had been a good plan.

how to do double knitting

To knit a pouch for a mobile phone like the one from the Lochranza workshop, cast on 30 stitches in Aran weight yarn with 4.5mm needles. You do not need double pointed knitting needles with this method but can knit a double sided piece on a pair of straight knitting needles.

Knit 1 slip 1 along the row. Slip the stitches purl-wise but with the yarn at the back.

Slip 1 knit 1 on the next row. The stitches that were knitted on row 1 are slipped on row 2 and vice versa.

Continue like this and after a few rows it will become more obvious which stitch is to be slipped and which knitted. The knitting will be two sided and if you pull the sides apart they will be separate from one another but be joined at the sides and bottom. You will find that you can slip one stitch and knit the next all in one motion and it takes half the time to knit the pouch if you do this. Try it and see – it's easy.

Once the pouch is long enough, slide every other stitch onto a third needle. This means it is now open at the top. Cast off one side. Continue to knit the other side a bit longer to make a flap then cast off.

Thanks to Louise at Woolfish who first introduced me to double knitting. I worked out the slip-and-knit-at-the-same-time thing though and we did think about jointly producing a video about it. Maybe one day...

Fig. 19: camera pouch made with double knitting

day 6, Saturday 4th July: Tarbert to Lochgilphead, 14 miles

Pam at Lochranza had predicted that the gales and heavy rain would ease during the morning. I took my time therefore, setting off at 11am with only light rain and no wind, to cycle the final mile into Tarbert and have a look at the Seafood Festival.

Artist Stuart Herd was doing caricatures to raise money for the festival and as the rain had come on again I ducked into his gazebo and had a sketch done of me on the bike. He had no fixative for the chalks he was using, so I nipped to the chemist for him and bought some hairspray, which worked very well.

It was raining even more by the time he had finished, so I crossed the road to a cafe and spent another hour having a slow lunch, before finally setting off for Lochgilphead at 1pm in light drizzle. It was an almost completely flat run along the edge of the sea – bliss after the hills of Arran. This was the third day of cycling in a row and I was pleased with how I was holding up, although a bit saddle sore.

Fig. 20: a caricature at Tarbert

There was no tent proofer to be had in Lochgilphead, because the fishing shop had forgotten to order it. I managed to buy tent pegs and found three guy ropes at the side of the road, so now had enough storm guys to keep the tent secure in most weather. There was nothing more to be done about it until I met up with Lee in Oban, when he would bring proofer with him.

There was no alternative but to get accommodation again. I booked into the Empire Travel Lodge Bed and Breakfast and was quite happy to do so, as the weather had got worse, with heavy showers and thunder. The Empire was a quirky place in an old cinema – hence the name – and used to belong to Jim's parents before he and Ele took it over. It had a trip advisor certificate of excellence and its own wee bistro, which was cheap and good. The room was four times the size of the last one at Tarbert and half the price. Ele even offered to do laundry for me – every cyclist's dream.

Although always chipper when on the bike, the B&B felt a bit lonely that night and a social plan was needed for any future rest days. Sitting crocheting in a hotel room all day, or in a tent zipped up against the weather was just no fun.

I looked up the local Quaker meeting which turned out to be back in Tarbert and got in touch. Edna and Bobby arranged to pick me up the following morning and take me to Tarbert for the meeting. Then, happy that there was a plan in place, I had a really deep bath and spent the evening finishing the crocheted tree. My first piece of completed crochet. Six days and I had finished one 30cm high crocheted tree – hardly impressive.

There was not too much knitting and crochet going on here and I was in a bit of a time crunch, what with the cycling, writing, knitting and crocheting, workshops, blogging, Facebook updates, eating and sleeping. And when camping, every basic thing took twice as long. The continued lack of a good phone signal bothered me more than I thought it would and was just one of several reminders that we are powerless over many things. By standing outside on the pavement it was just possible to phone Lee and have a brief chat.

Anyhow, the plans had been successfully adjusted to take account of the weather and I was warm, dry and grateful. I had this mental picture of sitting in the doorway of the tent in the evenings and crocheting whilst chatting with other campers. Apart from the first two nights at Kildonan on Arran, it was actually not until reaching Dingwall that this was to happen again, because of the midges, which were worse everywhere due to high rainfall. Even in Dingwall, I sat in the doorway of the tent and crocheted midge-free but in torrential rain.

day 7, Sunday 5th July: a visit to the Quaker meeting in Tarbert and a day off from cycling

a few coincidences

There had been quite a few coincidences whilst planning Knit 1 Bike 1 and on the journey itself. Things just kept appearing when they were needed. In other words, the world was carrying on as normal but I was noticing things more because of not being in a hurry and having a calmer mind.

Synchronicity is on the border between the credible and incredible so far as I am concerned, but it felt fine being alone. I surprised myself by being confident and not the slightest bit scared, believing things would go right and that people would be friendly and help.

Fig. 21: Ele and Jim at the Empire Travel Lodge

Drivers were courteous and I got cheery waves from cars. Folk stopped to chat and offered to lend a hand. Cafes produced cups of tea free of charge and sometimes even whole meals. That feeling of optimism persisted throughout trip - a reminder that most people are decent and well meaning and that we live in a great and safe country.

As far as the synchronicity thing went, here are some examples. When I needed something to wedge behind the rear rucksack so that it did not catch on my heels, it took all of ten minutes to spot a piece of polystyrene just the right size at the side of the road. I needed three additional guy ropes for the storm guy points on the tent and found all three just lying on the verge. They were a bit grubby but washed up great. I needed a waterproof phone case and - wonder of wonders - the plastic sleeve that the new tent pegs came in was perfect. It was even possible to use the touch screen buttons on the phone through the plastic. It was every bit as good as the posh purpose-made one Justine had on her front bike bag (which I had eyed enviously).

What caused me to think about all that was a change of plan due to the leaky tent. It had meant cancelling the following night's dinner with Sally from Kilmartin House Museum. Instead of camping in the grounds of the Museum and having dinner with Sally after the workshop, I would have to continue straight on to Oban. Then I could spend a dry night in the caravan with Lee and would have a free day to waterproof the tent. I had been so looking forward to the meal with Sally though and was sorry to miss it.

Fig. 22: the crocheted tree

But I walked around a corner in Lochgilphead, looking for somewhere to eat and there was Sally, the day *before* our dinner date. She was on her way to an Indian restaurant with her sister and their respective partners. So I joined them and we got to have dinner together after all.

Tarbert Quaker meeting

In the morning, before all that happened though, Edna and Bobby came to collect me and we headed off to Tarbert Quaker meeting. What a lovely couple and it was an enjoyable morning at the Meeting, with lots of snacks afterwards. Yes - food was a big thing throughout the journey – a cyclist's prerogative.

But then food is also a bit of a thing whenever cyclists, knitters, spinners or Quakers get together. One of the great things about all four of those interests is that you could go anywhere in the world and meet people with whom you had something in common. And be assured of getting lots to eat because they know food breaks the ice like nothing else.

Connecting through the things I had in common with others was partly what made the project such fun, and certainly that weekend I had been glad not to spend Sunday alone. Lochgilphead was mostly shut for business and the rain was heavy for much of the day. It would have meant a lot of time alone in a hotel room.

day 8, Monday 6th July: Lochgilphead to Kilmartin, 11 miles

workshop number 3

106 miles of cycling and proud to have made it this far. This was now my longest ever cycle trip. Both of the others had been over ten years ago and for a few days only but had followed a similar route as far as Tarbert.

Kilmartin House Museum is a favourite place and their shop stocks my craft kits and weaving. The museum itself has exhibits you can actually touch, a varied workshop programme with courses ranging from crafts to Permaculture, a fabulous cafe and an ecological slant to everything. Kilmartin is in an 'archaeological valley' and there is an exceptional range of burial mounds and standing stones in the field behind the museum. You can actually get right down inside the burial chambers.

Sally had organised things well, with posters all around Lochgilphead and an article in the local paper. Local newspapers are as much a part of rural life in Scotland as the ferries and cover many local events such as sheep dog trials, Highland games and of course Knit 1 Bike 1 workshops. I called in to see the Argyllshire Advertiser at their office in Lochgilphead before setting off and was interviewed and photographed on the spot.

Eight people attended the workshop which took place in a gazebo in the museum's grounds. Most wanted to learn to crochet and they were an enthusiastic bunch who knew how to enjoy themselves. The cafe brought out orders of tea and their legendary hot chocolate, which was as thick as syrup. There was much hilarity and in the midst of it all, Lee arrived, wearing a big smile and clutching the box containing all the things I had knitted and crocheted before leaving home.

The crocheted Isle of Mull ferry was a hit, as was the tree I had made on the way. Sally put a set of kitchen tongs into a teapot and put the tree over them so that everyone could see it. Eventually it would be stuffed and stiffened so that it could stand up properly but not until I got back home.

The curator had hinted that they would issue a challenge to me to crochet a life-sized replica of the largest, seven-foot-high standing stone in the stone circle behind the museum. Whether or not that came to pass, I agreed to crochet smaller versions of the stones as part of the exhibition.

Fig. 23: the workshop at Kilmartin

Lee was on his way to Oban and had come via the museum on his way there. So with me feeling like a bit of a cheat, I accepted a lift. But I was also relieved that the tent would finally get sorted before I set off for Mull.

We headed for Oban in a torrential downpour, towing our wee micro caravan. Lee cooked tea and I fell asleep quickly in the familiar surroundings of the caravan, listening to the heavy rain outside once again. Who knew so many adventures could be had practically on your own doorstep.

day 9, Tuesday 7th July: something may have changed forever...

Meeting up with Lee again caused me to notice I was less flustered by small things. For instance, taking a wrong turn with the caravan the day before had been no big deal and I was more able to take the longer view, knowing it would work out fine. I had dealt with problems on my own, without phoning home but also had the courage to ask for help when necessary – what a surprise, I was not so much of a wimp after all.

What had done it was this:

- Doing the adventurous (and let's face it, fairly daft) thing.
- Doing what needed to be done – writing the book, doing the crochet and putting in the miles.
- Connecting with others and having a plan to make that happen – ie mini workshops, staying with people and chatting in cafes.

My mind, meanwhile, had been pondering this:

- Was that microwavable container worth carrying? I really liked it because of the waterproof seal on the lid. It was filled with oatcakes but an awkward shape to pack and not much use for anything else.
- Was it worth carrying the sandals, given the weather?
- Was it worth buying another Spork when really a plain old metal spoon would do the job? I bought one anyway because they seemed more glamorous and came in pretty colours.
- How good it was not to have great big, complicated things to think about

I reluctantly let go of the sandals, along with some spare yarn. When combined with all the things that were posted home from Arran that made quite a difference. The bag did shut better but it really just meant I could carry more food, far more important than sandals but about the same as yarn...

day 10, Wednesday 8th July: the Island of Mull, Craignure to Tobermory, 24.5 miles

There was the threat of a strike by Caledonian MacBrayne ferry workers on Friday. The strike was about the government's intention to put this crucial service out to contract by compulsory competitive tender. It would change Scotland forever and in other areas such as the Isle of Man, had led to an inferior service, according to some.

I had crossed to Mull from Oban at 7.30 am. Now the trip became a whistle-stop tour, to avoid making the return crossing on the Friday. There would be two workshops at opposite ends of the island on consecutive days. I would have one overnight stay rather than two and arrive back in Oban a day earlier, on Thursday.

Lee had crossed over to Mull at the same time as me but was now on the opposite side of the island. Our granddaughter - called Skye - lived at Fionnphort on the far side of Mull and he was taking her down to her dad's in Paisley for the school holidays.

Fig. 24: road signs on Mull were a bit different

The day's 24.5 mile cycle was a little daunting, especially after hearing how steep the single track road was beyond Salen, going towards Tobermory. The road also had a reputation for being used as a racetrack by local youths, but I cycled it twice and it was fine. There was a passing place every 300 metres or so and cars could be heard for miles. It would have been easy to get out of the way had there been a speedy youngster approaching. Not that there were any.

It was a most enjoyable ride and I cycled from the ferry to Tobermory plus another 1.5 miles or so further on to the campsite. It was a bit of a nature trip because, being early in the morning, there were more creatures about. I rescued a toad and then rescued a baby field mouse that had fallen off a bank and got stuck at the side of the road.

Sadly a baby rabbit with a nasty facial injury was beyond saving. I managed to put it out of its misery, but that brought back losing our dear wee miniature poodle Freddie, who had been put down the year before. I cycled along a bit tearful for a few miles, wishing there was someone to talk to but it soon passed.

As a result of all this and some photography, it took two hours to cover the ten miles to Salen, then of course I stopped at a cafe for a cuppa and a wee snack. True Knit 1 Bike 1 style cycling, in other words.

The road to Tobermory was indeed a strenuous cycle but nothing compared to Arran, and the view from the top made it all worthwhile. It is the main thoroughfare on Mull, the A848, but it is narrow with passing places from Salen onwards. It was a bit surreal to meet a double decker bus coming the other way on a single track road.

Fig. 25: the bus from Tobermory

I found the campsite and pitched the tent before setting off back into Tobermory to get some food and later deliver the evening's workshop at An Tobar Arts Centre. Dinner was posh fish and chips from a van on Tobermory pier. They actually had a Les Routiers listing and reckoned they were the only fish and chip van to have it. As well as the usual fare, there were scallops, halibut and calamari, all of course in batter and served with chips. I chose the calamari and it was truly delicious.

Fig. 26: fish & chips with a Les Routiers award

Tobermory is a cosmopolitan and arty town. The main street has the famous multi-coloured buildings which probably inspired the set of the Scottish children's TV programme Ballamory. When I was cycling into Tobermory, a guy in a Range Rover stopped and asked me the way to Ballamory, then looked rather embarrassed when he realised what he had said. He was taking the kids, who were fans of the programme, to see the famous street.

Fig. 27: the colourful buildings in Tobermory

There were art galleries and shops like the Otter Trust and Whale and Dolphin Rescue. Considering the population of the whole island was only 5,000, it supported some great shops. There were lovely knitted whales and dolphins in the window of the Rescue shop and I bought some to include in the Knit 1 Bike 1 exhibition. They turned out to be knitted by a member of the group I was due to visit, but sadly she was away on holiday.

Fig. 28: the Whale and Dolphin Trust, Tobermory

workshop Number 4: An Tobar Arts Centre

The Woolly Wednesdays group met regularly at An Tobar. Helen and group organiser Dawn had asked me to come and teach them spindle spinning. I had taught Helen to spin a few years ago and she now had her own business, Helbies Handmade, selling hand spun yarns and other goodies at craft fairs and farmers markets.

It was lovely to see her again and to meet the eight other members of the group. They were an eclectic bunch, some born and bred on Mull, others who had moved there from the mainland or from South of the border and one member who lived there for only part of the year. Everyone got stuck in with great enthusiasm and did very well in the two hours, all going home with a wee length of their own handspun yarn.

It seemed a long way back up the hill to the campsite. There were fewer midges than at Lochranza on Arran though (actually, nowhere had as many midges as Lochranza). I felt like a real camper for the first time, getting the tent up in less than 15 minutes and even remembering where everything was.

Fig. 29: the workshop at An Tobar Arts Centre

It rained heavily during the night and finally the tent was truly waterproof. Hooray! At an initial cost of £345, I would need to sleep in it for at least 12 nights in order for it to earn its keep, and this was only the fourth night of camping so far.

the Highland midge

For the benefit of those who have not experienced them, midges are tiny, do not carry disease and do no lasting damage - but their bites sting and itch. Because of their sheer numbers, you can quickly become hysterical without a midge net and a midge-free tent to escape to.

Some people pretend they are not bothered by them, but they have just not camped on Skye on a muggy July night, when the whole of the tent can become black with literally millions of them. Midges tend to go to bed once the sun comes out, a bit like vampires, really...

A midge net is the only thing that really works when there are millions of midges on a dull morning or evening. Do not go into the hills without one. We once climbed Goat Fell, a mountain on Arran and got to the top to find about twenty people there admiring the view, which was a bit of a surprise. We were the only ones with midge nets and could have sold any spare ones for a king's ransom. Oh – and don't wear shorts.

a typical cycle-camping Knit 1 Bike 1 day

Wake early and with good intentions. Spend some time trying not to need the loo before it gets truly light and the midges die down. Put on the midge net and dive frantically out of the tent, hopefully without letting too many of them in. Off to the loo block for a wash and brush up, using as little of the precious sliver of soap and tiny jar of moisturiser as possible.

Zip the tent up firmly then spend ten minutes killing the midges that have, inevitably, got in. Put on the slightly damp clothes washed the night before and eat some oatcakes and apples for breakfast. Then write, crochet or knit until the sun gets brighter or a breeze starts up, so that the tent can be packed away without the midges for company. Feel efficient and just a tiny bit smug at having managed all this so well, and start packing up the gear. This quickly becomes a fiasco and takes up to another hour and a half. Fiddle with the rear bag in order to get it to sit just right and not catch on my heels.

Check the map several times, set off, stop and start again in order to adjust the luggage before finally getting under way. Stop every few minutes to take photographs and rescue wildlife before realising it has taken an hour to cycle five miles. Resolve to press on. Cycle proudly up almost every hill and think how fit I am, not that it makes me go any faster. Stop for tea at the first cafe and never go past it, because who knows when there will be another? Fail to resist things that are bad for me.

Eat lunch at the roadside from what I have with me, or buy food in local shops. Arrive at the campsite, house or B&B by about 3pm. Have a shower, eat lots of food and repair the rear pannier yet again. Spend time writing, blogging and going through the day's photographs. So much to do, so little time...

and here's what I had learned:

- Wearing your knickers inside out means the gusset does not rub. Vaseline is my friend.
- Carrying cold food works but it would be really nice to have more cups of tea.

- There are not always handy coffee shops and eating out all the time quickly becomes tedious, expensive and unhealthy.
- I am not very good at setting off early unless I have to, although I go to bed every night with good intentions.
- Everything takes longer in a tent. Finding things in the half-light of a tent by rummaging in a dark coloured bag, when you cannot stand up, is a tad frustrating.
- It is just as hard to finish knitting and crochet projects whilst on the road as it is at home and there is always something else that needs doing.

day 11, Thursday 9th July: Tobermory back to Craignure, on to Loch Don, back to Craignure yet again, then over to Oban, 27.5 miles - phew!

thermals in July

Even wearing everything I had, it was not warm enough to get a really good night's sleep. It was still the best night's sleep in the tent so far though, as I had now calmed down and was not so overexcited.

Fortunately, Lee had brought the thermal undershirt back up to Oban. I had also bought a pair of tights to wear if it got really cold. At this stage, I still thought the nights would get warmer but they never did and you could see your breath in the morning. Despite being in a hurry, or maybe because of it, setting off took ages.

Staying in the tent till 9am to avoid the midges was a good plan though and they had mostly gone by the time I got the gear packed up. There was a kettle under a canopy on the site and I made porridge in the plastic microwavable container with boiling water. It was not enough to fill me up though and now there was washing up to do, with no tea towel or cloth. So oatcakes and fruit remained a better option.

There was a bit of urgency as I needed to cycle back to Craignure, then on to Loch Don in order to give another workshop there at 4pm. After finally setting off at 10.40, I made good progress until going wrong at the roundabout only a mile and a half later and just outside Tobermory.

Fig. 30: on the road from Tobermory to Loch Don

Instead of staying on the high road, I whizzed half a mile down an almost vertical hill into the town itself. I had not intended to stop in the town again, but seeing as I was there anyway, took photos of the brightly coloured buildings and looked at the shops before pushing the bike back up the hill, which was way too steep for cycling.

Having just got underway, I realised how hungry I was and tackling ten miles of hills on an empty stomach was just not going to work. Stopping at a seafood place for sustenance, I ate as fast as possible setting off – for real this time – at 12.00. I was feeling rather rushed and kept thinking "proper cyclists don't do this". But then neither do they have so much fun and knit on the way. It was a hard ride back to Salen and at the top of the hill, who should I meet but Lee and Skye making their way to Tobermory for a look around.

Lee took the rear bag, because he was bringing Skye to the workshop at Loch Don later on and I continued with a slightly lighter load. It was only after he had gone that I realised he had the bag containing the trousers and tee shirt I needed to change into for the workshop.

At Salen I stopped on a bench outside the church to eat lunch, resisting another cafe stop this time. I was finally learning where to find benches – outside churches, in community gardens and in parks. And failing that, sit in a bus stop.

workshop number 5: Loch Don, Mull

Liz Gibson's croft was 2.5 miles beyond the ferry terminal and she grew connoisseur tea, which cost £35 for a wee packet. There is a whole world of speciality tea like this apparently and it is marketed by www.weeteacompany.com. Who knew you could grow tea in the UK? I ordered a tea bush from Margaret at Plants With Purpose, because they were on the Knit 1 Bike 1 itinerary and I would be visiting them when I got to Dunkeld.

We all had a cup of Liz's delicate stem tea at the workshop which was absolutely delicious and bore no relation at all to ordinary black tea. The four people who attended were all keen knitters, including a WWOOF volunteer (World Wide Opportunities on Organic Farms) who was staying at the croft to help with the gardening.

A happy couple of hours was spent showing people how to do mattress stitch, which, for the non knitters amongst us, joins two pieces of knitting with a flat and almost invisible seam. We also did some double knitting and Lee and Skye joined us for an hour.

Skye had been learning to knit every time she came down to Ayrshire to stay with us. I was a proud granny as she sat there doing her knitting along with everyone else. Then she collected some eggs from Liz's hens for us to take back to Oban. Skye had been the only one in her class who could not knit – no wonder she was keen to learn. It highlighted what a different culture there was on Mull compared to most mainland schools, where even the teacher often cannot knit these days.

In true Island fashion, Liz, Sue and Susan had fun working out who Skye's mum Leigh was. They all knew of Skye even though they had not met her before and they asked after her wee sister Ruby and brother Angus.

I had been looking forward to a lift back to the ferry after that super high-speed cycle from Tobermory to Loch Don, 21.5 miles in 3 hours, mostly up hill. Well, speedy for me anyway. But I had forgotten that Lee's van only had two seats in it and Skye was coming back to Oban with us. So it was back on the bike and a 2.5 mile trudge to Craignure. Only to find that the following day's strike had been called off and I could have had a comfy night at Liz's and a rest after all.

Fig. 31: the workshop at Loch Don

At the other side, there was another 1.5 miles up hill from Oban back to the campsite where we had left the caravan. It was my turn to go on strike, refusing to cycle another inch and I drove the van whilst Lee cycled the bike for the final stretch. I fell into bed in the caravan after a hot shower and rather a lot of food, and had the best night's sleep since setting off.

day 12, Friday 10th July: three miles from the campsite to Oban and back

Twelve days and it seemed like life had been this way forever. After the last two days on Mull I had been a bit stiff but better than expected. Mull was a demanding ride and the cycling had been faster because of the time constraints. Christine, who had done a spindling course with me at the Edinburgh Yarn Festival, got in touch to say she was up in Oban on holiday and did I fancy a coffee? Of course I did and she insisted on treating me to breakfast. I wolfed it down hungrily, realising only once I had finished that Christine was watching me patiently and only had a piece of toast herself, having already breakfasted at the hotel. I did have muesli before setting out but was still ravenous after the previous two days of cycling.

We had a lovely knitting chat – the kind of talk I had hungered for since parting from Justine on day two. The workshops were short and there had not been much time to just hang out, drink coffee and chat, a favourite way of mine to pass the time.

We had fun talking to a couple at the next table. The guy had the largest rucksack I had ever seen and we just had to ask him about it. He sounded Canadian and was planning to walk the West Highland Way, saying he needed to carry a lot because it would take three weeks. Hopefully there were no boggy sections or he would sink. I could not even lift the rucksack off the floor and we took a picture of him with his monstrous burden. What I really wanted to ask is whether he had a midge net in there...

Christine presented me with a beautiful Fair Isle hand knitted purse, filled with all kinds of knitting goodies. I went on to look around the shops a bit more after we said goodbye, finally tracking down the Activist Cafe someone had mentioned. I wanted to visit and tell them about Knit 1 Bike 1.

Fig. 32: Christine at Oban

The Activist Cafe was staffed by volunteers and you could make a donation for tea and cake, or just hang out there. A young couple from Edinburgh came in. They were motor biking and wild camping for a few days. We had some great 'activist' chat and they promised to wave and hoot if they passed me the following day. They did, and went past waving and tooting madly.

Community and church cafes were the secret to budget travel, I was to discover later on. They were invariably hard to find and you needed to ask around, but for cheap food and somewhere to sit in the rain, they were the best.

Fig. 33: you are going where with that?

day 13, Saturday 11th July: Oban to Fort William, 15 miles cycling and a bus ride

rain, rain and more rain

Citylink buses were great and ran all over Scotland. You could get a ticket sent to your phone and although you could just show up, booking guaranteed a seat. On the bus from Oban to Ballachulish, the driver carefully stowed the bike and bags in the hold and the whole thing was a lot easier than getting on a train.

By the time we got to Ballachulish, the rain was really heavy. The bus had dropped me at the side of the road, disorientated and with not much in sight other than the bus stop. There was a tourist information centre across the road, seemingly in the middle of nowhere although actually it was on the edge of the village. I grabbed the bags, intending to attach them to the bike in the shelter of their front canopy. It was a good move because it turned out they also had a cafe serving huge breakfasts. So I sat for an hour, ate scrambled eggs and beans, wrote and waited for the rain to ease up.

The journey from Ballachulish to Fort William meant cycling along the A82. There was a cycle track along about half of it but after that it was challenging. Eventually I discovered the traffic came in clumps and would watch for it in the rear view mirror, pull off the road and wait for it to pass, cycling along in relative tranquility. This worked on every busy road thereafter.

Fig. 34: the tent drying on Morag's kitchen table

The rain continued and the plan was to camp in Fort William and then go to Morag's in Lochailort the following day. When I phoned to confirm arrangements though, she immediately invited me to come a night earlier. I did not need asking twice as another night of camping in torrential rain did not appeal. As Morag was coming to Fort William to do her shopping, she insisted on giving me a lift as well. I had intended to get the train but it seemed churlish to muck up her plans.

It was wonderful being in a house in front of the wood stove. An evening of good conversation about everything from Gaelic, food, cats and knitting to the recent referendum on Scottish independence made a good evening perfect.

I drifted off to sleep in cotton sheets under a feather duvet, snug and warm and yet again listening to the rain outside. The tent meanwhile was draped over her dining room table to dry – it had not been possible to dry it out properly in the caravan and it was still as wet as when it had been packed up on Mull.

Fig. 35: Morag at her house at Lochailort

day 14, Sunday 12th July: a pyjama day

In the morning, the rain was still streaming down the windows and the wind was lashing the trees. Some catch-up time was sorely needed, especially on the crochet front, and there were a couple of spare days before the planned workshop on Tuesday with the Mallaig knitting group.

Being at Morag's also meant finally having an internet connection that actually worked, so I updated the blog and wrote an article for my publisher, The Low-impact Living Initiative (lowimpact.org), to put on *their* blog.

The fast cycle the day before and the hills on Mull had caught up with me and although the stiffness had worn off, the tiredness had not. I eventually succumbed and had a nap. Naps became a regular feature of the Knit 1 Bike 1 day from then on. I would cycle, then have forty winks on arriving at a destination, before taking on the rest of the day.

The crochet progressed well for once and there were a dozen or so crocheted mussel shells, some seaweed and part of a rock to show for it. So a thoroughly lazy time but not *really* a pyjama day because I did not have any pyjamas, just the one tee shirt for use day and night. I had sent the other one home and forgotten I would need it on the non-cycling days. Just as well I had that long sleeved merino undershirt with me.

day 15, Monday 13th July: 8 miles – an artistic visit

A wee trip to see artist Alison Durbin. She lived a few miles away from Morag, in a state of the art wooden house with attached studio. She and her partner had created it, project managing the building work themselves. Alison did all kinds of things, from printing to willow work and her partner led workshops in woodland and outdoor skills. It was helpful to chat with a fellow artist and exchange ideas.

Fig. 36: Alison Durbin at Wildwood

I have a qualification in spinning and another in crochet, both of which involved design and portfolio work, but I did not go to art school and sometimes feel the lack of it. Part of the reason for the Knit 1 Bike 1 project was to take the time to do some creative work, writing and photography. At home I was often too busy delivering workshops to actually make things, or to study method and technique. The project was a chance to play and to make things that were 'art' rather than useful. Crocheting and knitting everything from the Glenfinnan Viaduct to worms and a road would certainly qualify.

Alison suggested photographing some of the work in nature and on the way back I got some pictures of the crocheted mussel shells and rocks on the beach of Loch Ailort. It was a sea loch and therefore tidal with seaweed and beaches at low tide. As Alison pointed out, photographs of artists' work are often offered for sale at exhibitions, something I had not considered. A useful day and a good reminder to focus on the earning potential of the proposed exhibition, as well as that of the book. After all even artists have to eat.

Time at Morag's to re-group and adjust to life away from home had been useful. What must it be like being a refugee living in a tent all year round? It took so much energy just to survive, to cook, get water and stay clean.

Fig. 37: crocheted shells on the beach

day 16, Tuesday 14th July: Mallaig Craft Group

Morag and I went to Mallaig together and she gave me a lift, as we were going for fish and chips before the workshop. It was frustrating as the old legs needed a good stretch, but it was more sociable and made perfect sense. People often offered me lifts in their cars and I guess they thought it was somehow better than the bike or public transport. The cycling was a pleasure not a hardship though. There was so much more to see, it was easier to meet people and you are part of the surroundings. I saw things in villages and towns that even those who lived there often missed. On this occasion it was just sensible however.

The fish and chip shop was just a hole in the kitchen door of a local restaurant and quite famous locally. Mallaig is at the end of the steam train ride from Fort William so there were plenty of tourists there.

Fig. 38: the chip shop in the wall, Mallaig

We visited Ginger knitting design studio and had a cup of tea with the owner. She is called Anna but everyone just called her Ginger. There were some wonderful things for sale and when the steam train arrived, customers were shoulder to shoulder in her wee shop. Anna gave me some lovely sand and beach coloured yarns for the project and joined us for the crochet workshop later on.

Fig. 39: Ginger Knitting Studio, Mallaig

There were twelve people at the workshop and enough cake for thirty of us. It was a good laugh and a challenge was issued for me to crochet the large strawberry sponge cake on the table, which I duly did. Morag was delighted when I posted a picture of it on Facebook later and said she would show it to the group. They presented me a thank you card depicting Elvis Presley and a generous donation towards Knit 1 Bike 1 at the end of the evening.

day 17, Wednesday 15th July: train to Glenfinnan, cycle to (almost) Fort William, 17 miles

It was great to be on the road again and use those legs. And what a day. It started with the train from Lochailort to Glenfinnan, which cut nine miles' cycling off the journey to Fort William. The station was close to the now-famous Glenfinnan Viaduct featured in the Harry Potter films. A steam train arrived at the same time and there was a harpist and all sorts of people milling about in kilts.

Fig. 40: Mallaig knitting group

After cycling for a while on the A82 from Glenfinnan towards Fort William, I took the lovely Strontian road. A five minute ferry crossing from Camusnagaul to Fort William made this route possible and it was popular with cyclists. I took my time and enjoyed the view, even stopping to update the blog on the way. Then suddenly I was running out of time to catch the 12.30 ferry!

Despite cycling like mad, I missed the ferry by a whisker and the next one was not until 4.30. Whilst having a snack and weighing up the options, a bus came along. I leaped out and flagged it down, asking the driver if he was going back to the main A82. He said yes although he did look a bit bemused.

Fig. 41: the crocheted cake on its plate

I asked him to wait for me to fold the bike up and he smiled, saying it could just travel like it was. It was only once I was aboard that it became obvious this was not a service bus at all. It had been converted into a youth bus and mobile recording studio for the 'Buzz' youth Project!

That was all rather embarrassing but he did not mind at all and we had a great chat on the way. Actually, if he had happened along two minutes earlier he would have caught me having a rapid pee at the side of the road. There were no convenient bushes or trees so I had just waited till the road was clear and gone ahead.

Fig. 42: the steam train at Glenfinnan

The Buzz Project aims to reduce isolation amongst young people in the area, which has one of the highest suicide rates in Western Europe. The project coordinator was driving the bus and took me all the way to Fort William. I arrived there nice and early and had time to buy a new rucksack to replace the rear pannier before it fell to bits completely.

The outdoor shop staff were most helpful and did not flinch when I explained the need to unpack the old bag, repack everything in the new one and try it on the bike for size before buying it. They even disposed of the old one and I bought a couple of fancy karabiners as well, to attach the new rucksack to the saddle. The old bit of orange rope was still needed to prevent the rucksack from swinging from side to side, but it was a big improvement.

Fig. 43: the new rear rucksack at Fort William

A night in the tent and I was really getting the hang of it, choosing a good spot with plenty of light and fewer midges. The large campsite had great facilities, including a breakfast van, cafe and restaurant. After that super-speedy sprint for the ferry, I went a bit loopy with cakes in the cafe but had truly earned it and had *surely* burned off enough calories for some extra indulgence.

The domestic chores such as laundry, showering, packing and unpacking took less time than before and routines were getting easier. I loaded everything into a washing machine and waited on a comfy seat whilst reading a book and charging the mobile phone at the same time. It was bedtime by the time everything was more or less done though and yet again there was no time to crochet or knit.

day 18 Thursday 16th July – Fort William to Dalmally 12.5 miles cycling.

People on the campsite were fidgeting overnight because of the cold and at one point a couple started up their car to get warm, pouring exhaust fumes into my tent.

There was no choice other than to get up and suggest they take their sleeping bags into the laundry, which thankfully they did. I pulled the hood of the sleeping bag shut and burrowed down inside, wearing the tights, tee shirt, merino undershirt, fleece, trousers and two pairs of socks, with the waterproof jacket over the top.

Shutting the vents in the tent caused condensation so they had to be open a tiny bit, causing a draft round my head. How I missed the old Wynnster tent, even if it did weigh more. The readiness to rough it a bit was still there though and I did not fall apart like the couple in the car. I dozed whilst thinking 'it will pass and this is July so there is no risk of hypothermia.'

Having a Kindle app on the phone made a big difference. The app did not use much battery power and was back lit, making it possible to read in the dark and even with my head inside the sleeping bag. So when sleep did not come easily I read trashy knitting novels, such as the crime knitting series by Maggie Sefton and the Amish Knitting Circle series by Anna Vogel. It began to warm up at 6am and I got a couple of hours' decent sleep at last.

A chilly night was definitely better than midges and the Glen Nevis site had everything a camper could wish for. A cooked breakfast was a luxury well worth the money, and it was nice to have a comfy seat in the restaurant, bask in the warmth, and read for a while before setting off.

a train to Upper Tyndrum

Having a folding bike was a real advantage on trains because I could always get on no matter how many bikes were in front of me. Although people had booked their bikes on the train from Fort William to Upper Tyndrum, none of the seat or bicycle reservations had been processed due to 'staff shortages' so it was a bit of a free for all. The trains normally only took a limited number of bikes but everyone managed to squeeze on, including a tandem.

The Brompton could go in the luggage rack of course but I had booked it on as a 'bike' just in case. Not that it would have made any difference in the circumstances. As there was a great deal of luggage on the train, it went with the other bikes in the dedicated bike compartment and there was no need to take the front and rear bags off in order to fold it up.

Fig. 44: the crocheted limpets on a rock

A couple of young German cyclists on the train were good company and we managed to communicate quite well. They were cycle touring in Scotland for two weeks and the guy had previously cycled round Alaska. They had even heard of Knit 1 Bike 1, having picked up a leaflet on Skye - fame at last.

Fig. 45: crocheted Glenfinnan Viaduct in progress

The pair of them had rather rashly camped at Sligachan on Skye and they told me how their socks hung outside the tent overnight had become coated in such a thick layer of midges that it was impossible to see what colour they were. This is what people talked about everywhere: the trains and buses, the weather, food and the midges.

I finished the crocheted rocks with limpets whilst on the train and they were duly admired by fellow passengers, before being posted home from Dalmally. The Glenfinnan Viaduct was added to the 'must crochet or knit' list as the train travelled over it, but little did I know what a big job that would turn out to be!

There was a huge horizontal gap between the platform and the train at many of the old-fashioned Highland stations. This was because the platforms had not been adapted for modern trains and this was made worse by the fact that the train was also a lot *higher* than the platform.

I usually loaded the bike onto the train before taking the luggage off and folding it. I got stuck more than once with the bike halfway on, my arms not being long enough to push it on the rest of the way, or strong enough to lift it with the heavy luggage. It was tricky because the gap was so wide that the wee Brompton wheels would actually have gone down it. Someone always helped, although it was a bit scary at times. The trains were full of luggage and bikes and having worried about taking the Citylink bus, it was far easier than the trains, with a huge hold and a helpful driver to load bags and bike onto the coach.

Fig. 46: Liz, Sandra and Graham at Dalmally

The new rear luggage was easier to manage but it still took a good ten minutes to get it all back together at Upper Tyndrum. It was an easy twelve mile cycle from there to Dalmally on a wide, smooth road with little traffic and only gentle hills. I was going there to visit friend and feltmaker Liz Gaffney-Waite and her hubby-to-be Graham, arriving in the midst of preparations for their wedding, which was to take place a couple of weeks later.

An Irish welcome as ever at Liz's studio 'Heartfelt' and a great abundance of food and people, including Sandy and Jeanette. They had travelled there to meet up and do the wee Knit 1 Bike 1 crochet workshop the following day. I went to sleep in Liz and Graham's cosy shepherd's hut, feeling thoroughly well looked after and grateful for all the friends and textile artists who had offered me a bed for the night.

day 19, Friday 17th July: crocheted flowers at Dalmally

workshop number 7

At today's crocheted flowers workshop folks got quite creative, especially Sandy, whom I had first met when teaching her to spin a few of years before. She sold her work in Dunoon and planned to make brooches out of her lovely crocheted flowers. Liz and Graham live in the still-active railway station and the workshop was in a room opening off the platform. At one point Sandy dashed across the platform to the other side and delivered a spindle spinning kit to a guy in a passing train! Liz's pet lamb came and joined us for a while too.

Fig. 47: the workshop at Dalmally

It was good to catch up with old friends, spend time with Liz and get to know Graham, because I had only previously met him briefly. I ate and ate, convincing myself that I needed to make up for all that cycling, but the reality was this: I comfort ate a lot whilst travelling and more or less got away with it because of all the cycling. Being tired a lot of the time also made me crave cakes – i.e. sugar - more than I ever did at home. Drat the Highlands for having so many gluten free cakes available in cafes.

Fig. 47a: a lamb visits the workshop at Dalmally

I lay in bed that night thinking "this is me doing this journey" and it still did not feel very real. It was as if someone else was doing it and I was watching. But at the same time it had become familiar and was hard to believe I would ever be home again. After the first few days I asked Lee if we could speak most evenings, partly for the conversation but also to make sure someone actually knew I had arrived at that day's destination safely.

day 20, Saturday 18th July: Skye beckons...

Making it to Mallaig in time for the ferry to Skye meant getting the train from Dalmally, rather than cycling. I was retracing my steps by going back to Mallaig but after that I would be leaving familiar territory, which was exciting. The route back to Fort William and on to Mallaig left from Dalmally Station with a half mile cycle from Lower to Upper Tyndrum, then on to Fort William. So I simply hopped out of Liz and Graham's back door and onto the train.

The scenic West Highland line from Fort William to Mallaig is popular with tourists, especially since the Harry Potter books have been published. Many people on the train had just come for the ride on this beautiful, scenic route, planning to go there and back to Fort William on the same day. All the return trains were cancelled due to staff shortages though and they faced a long journey back by bus. It was lucky I had chosen an early train, as the outward trains from Fort William to Mallaig were also affected and mine was the last one to go. A steam train travelled the same line but I was on the regular Scotrail version. Yet again, the reservation tickets had not been put out on the seats and there was luggage everywhere. Rucksacks and holdalls were squashed in amongst the bicycles, which were suspended from the wall in a special hanging bike rack, although mine was folded up and tucked in a corner.

The two conductors ran the train with vigour and their sense of humour kept everyone in good spirits, with an almost carnival atmosphere and everyone chatting to each other. Anyone still grumpy about the lack of a seat reservation just looked like a spoilsport and soon cheered up. Some stations were request stops and had platforms shorter than the train, so everyone had to move forward to the front three coaches if they were getting off. It was all just very *Scottish* somehow and the kind of thing that those of us who live here take for granted. Touring on the bike was making me notice my own country.

At Mallaig, there was plenty of time to stock up on food at the Cooperative store. The campsite had advised that the Armadale shop closed at lunchtime on Saturdays and would not re-open until Monday, so this was important. There was also time to get a cup of tea in the Mission cafe, where I shared a table with a fellow cyclist and ordered a fresh crab sandwich having seen what his looked like.

The ferries had been cancelled all day due to high winds but luckily the 3.15 ran. It was fine so long as you remained seated but the sea was still high and walking about was like being on a bucking bronco. The wind was building up again and it turned out this was the only ferry to run, with later ones also being cancelled.

forest garden campsite

The Skye Forest Garden campsite was right by the ferry terminal at Armadale. It was quirky, unique and based on permaculture principles. There was no mains sewerage and it had excellent, home-built composting loos even for the stylish "eco pods" which were available to rent there. The site actively encouraged walkers and cyclists, with motor vehicles being parked in a designated area and a 50p discount for those who arrived on foot or by bicycle. It took tents only, no caravans allowed. All the pitches were in small woodland clearings, with fire pits, camp kitchens and composting loos dotted about in the woods. The pitches were amongst the trees and I was rather nervous about the midges. There was one space near the cliff top but with the wind still building up, an inland pitch was the way to go. It was quite a distance to push the bike along a woodland path, but well worth the effort.

As it happened, there were gales and heavy rain all night and the spot I chose was fine and cosy, if a tad muddy. The site had a lovely textile studio and there had been a dyeing workshop there the day before. Sandra who ran the project explained that the site was a registered charity and volunteers came to help with jobs.

confession time

I did have a bit of a wimpy moment just before coming to Skye. I had probably not been drinking enough water whilst cycling, partly due to anxieties about where to go to the loo. This anxiety, like so many, was unfounded, because there was usually a tearoom, hotel or public building with a loo and I was learning where to find them. I had also become good at finding a suitable bush and having a very quick pee before the next car came along!

The thing is, my pee was completely colourless and with a greasy layer floating on top. (Yuck - but it *is* one of those things cyclists think about). Panicking about kidney failure I phoned Lee who looked it up on NHS Online and reported that no, I would have been in pain and the "pee description" was classed as normal. It was only then that I remembered that Graham at Dalmally had supplied us with tea all day the day before – I had been drinking it non-stop. And using Vaseline on one's nether regions whilst cycling would no doubt have caused the oil slick. What it did tell me was that yes, I was being a bit neurotic but as with any paranoia it was based on a grain of truth. The fact that I had been avoiding drinking much whilst on the road must have been at the back of my mind.

I needed to make sure that I drank enough *and* ensure that I had something better to think about. So off I went to the pub for some fish, chips, diet coke and good company. Surprisingly I had discovered in myself the capacity to do just that during the cycle ride – switch off, use distraction and have fun. I was quite proud of being able to do it and let's face it, wallowing when you are alone is not sensible and there was little point anyway, with no one there to listen.

day 21, Sunday 19th July: Armadale to Ashaig via Broadford, 20 miles

There had been a continuing condensation problem in the tent. The previous night, I had by chance secured the centre pegs at either end last of all when pitching it, instead of doing them first. The tent pitched a whole lot better and there was now a wee gap between the fly sheet and the ground at the ends. The air circulation improved and voila – no more condensation. But why had the tent instructions and YouTube videos not said that? My Girl Guide training had told me to do the opposite, but tents had changed rather since then.

The camp kitchen beside the tent had no running water but was clean and well set up, with worktops and even a veranda and deck chairs. I made up sandwiches with the remaining food before setting off, having a nice chat with a couple of cyclists from Yorkshire at the same time. They had been stuck at Forest Garden for three days, waiting out the stormy island weather. I rather envied their colourful dri-bags but hey, plastic bags worked okay - except for the rustling when packing up early in the morning. And the tendency to get tiny holes in them. It was only later on that I was to discover the delights of such hi-tech equipment for myself. They had not been so readily available during my previous forays into cycle camping ten years before, but now almost everyone had them.

Although there had been such a lovely atmosphere in the Forest Garden campsite the day before, a night of heavy rain had turned it rather muddy. Volunteers had strewn bracken on the mud but it was still good to get out into the open. The seventeen mile cycle to Broadford was hard work, with long, steady hills for the first fourteen miles or so and a strong head wind. I stopped at a church in the middle of nowhere having heard singing and just stood outside in the sunshine and listened for a while.

There were no cafes at all on the way and it was a relief to finally spot the one at the Reptile Centre just outside Broadford. My sandwiches were long gone and I sorely needed a comfy seat. Their homemade tomato soup and gluten-free brownies were delicious, but then again, just dry bread would probably have been delicious, as I was so hungry.

Fig. 48: the Help for Heroes walker at Broadford

Outside the cafe was a guy who was walking round Britain to raise money for Help For Heroes. He had been on the road for fifteen months and had walked fourteen thousand miles, with another eighteen thousand still to go. And here was I thinking ten weeks was a long time to be away from home. I wondered what his story was and whether he would ever be able to settle in one place as a civilian.

Knit 1 Bike 1 is here...

A final mile took me into Broadford to check out the Handspinner Having Fun, the yarn shop venue for the following day's workshop. There on the roadside was a lovely big notice saying "Knit 1 Bike 1 coming here on 20th July!". Having started the day a bit blue because of all that rain and mud, it had been a wonderful ride in sunshine, fun meeting the Help for Heroes guy at the cafe and now this – wow.

Mel at the Ashaig campsite a couple of miles the other side of Broadford was looking out for me. He announced that Bev from the

Handspinner had paid the campsite fees, as well as inviting me round for dinner the following night.

Fig. 49: the Knit 1 Bike 1 sign at Broadford

There was a large notice saying the site was full, but in common with all the other campsites except for Blair Atholl, it had a policy of never turning backpackers or cyclists away. The site had all mod cons including a residential caravan which had been converted into a day room, with a kettle, comfy seats, a ping pong table and somewhere to charge the phone up.

I rather guiltily appreciated the flush toilets and hot shower, feeling I ought to have liked the composting loos at the Forest Garden better. Actually, the composting ones were fine. They were well set up, perfectly clean and odour free, with soap and water for washing. Sometimes camping just felt like hard work though, without anything extra to consider.

food and drink

Not carrying a cooker saved weight and so far buying food from local Co-ops or eating out had worked reasonably well, although it was to increasingly become a challenge as time went on. The wind and rain would have made it impossible to use the camping stove anyway.

At Broadford, the artisan bakery next to Bev's shop sold gluten-free bread and with a tub of egg mayo, apples and cucumber it made a feast that evening. Spork number two had broken in half when I forgot it was in my pocket, but the remaining half still worked okay as a spoon. The wee collapsible silicon cup came into its own and it was nice to brew a cup of tea at the campsite to wash it all down with.

Fig. 50: campsite full at Ashaig near Broadford

All those convenience foods we avoided at home such as pre-cut carrots and tubs of salad were just great for camping. For the duration of the trip I ignored the fact that they all came in disposable plastic packaging and were three times the price.

what was I crocheting?

The crochet project in progress was the Cuillins of course - that mountain range that gives the island of Skye its distinctive profile. I worked from a couple of photos and a postcard and used some chunky multicoloured yarn called "Rico Creative Melange Chunky" which was just the right shade. Oh, and I had now been away for three whole weeks, which was one week more than ever before. Feeling very grown up.

day 22, Monday 20th July: Ashaig to Broadford and back, 6 miles

Eventually I set off for the Handspinner at 12.30 having spent the morning doing goodness knows what. Time just seemed to pass like that in the tent. I would spend the morning thinking about nothing in particular, or deciding whether to have a cup of tea. Maybe camping in a muddy field simply gives us back that in-between time where not very much happens. It allows us just to be, instead of always having to do something useful. Whenever I had watched the local ospreys on a webcam near home they seemed to be doing the same thing – just hanging out. And the time seemed to drift gently by – lovely.

workshop number 8: the Handspinner Having Fun

The Handspinner Having Fun is a yarn shop in a wonky little row of prettily painted corrugated iron shops, by the old harbour in Broadford. Bev took it on a year ago and had enthusiastically prepared for the Knit 1 Bike 1 workshop, including the roadside sign, balloons and an article in the local paper.

Fig. 51: the Handspinner Having Fun at Broadford

Fourteen enthusiastic women turned up to the workshop. It was on continental knitting, where you hold the yarn in the left hand instead of the right, like us Brits tend to do. It is particularly useful when doing coloured knitting as you can hold one colour of yarn in each hand and work with them both in turn at great speed. Most UK knitters find it easier and faster on knit rows than purl rows and we experimented with different ways of doing the purl rows.

The women then got stuck into Bev's lovely yarns, buying all sorts of things. Spending the afternoon sitting amongst it all with plenty of time to look around probably helped. I had been having sock knitting withdrawal, so bought some silk hand dyed sock yarn – very similar to that which I dyed myself back home but I did not have any with me. And the fact that I too had spent the afternoon sitting amongst it all just may have had something to do with it.

stormy weather

Afterwards, I cycled to Bev's house for dinner in torrential rain. The rain continued all night and by the time I got back to the tent the wind was howling and it was really rather wild. I double pegged the tent, made sure the storm guys were secure and got up a couple of times during the night to check it over. Nothing had budged and all the pegs were secure, so I went to sleep happy in the knowledge that the tent would still be there in the morning. I did wake up at 4am and take a video of the inside of the tent being buffeted by the wind. Amazingly, there was a mobile signal for once so I uploaded it to Facebook. Lee was very impressed when he saw it in the morning. There were several tents adrift by the morning but I was pleased with the performance of mine and forgave it all its previous shortcomings.

day 23, Tuesday 21ˢᵗ July: Broadford to Plockton, 14 miles

a change of plan

Lee (a.k.a. mission control) reported that the wind was to be even worse by the following night and already a fierce gale was blowing. It was impossible to cycle against it towards Uig, and the ferry to Harris would not be running anyway. So Lee, with his reliable internet signal at home, booked me a Bed and Breakfast in Plockton and I cycled a very fast five miles to the Skye bridge with the wind behind me and then up the coast to Plockton. Once on the mainland, the wind died down and the sun was out in Plockton, which had its own micro climate. People were even wearing shorts there.

The bay at Plockton was full of yachts which stayed there for three days just like me, as the weather continued to be stormy on the islands and outside the bay. I had one night at Mackenzie's B&B, right on the sea front but decided to stay a couple more days as I had some spare time due to missing out Harris and Lewis. In other words I had a holiday.

The B&B had a bath and I plunged into the really hot water, steaming up the bathroom and staying there for an hour, before finally emerging all pink and wrinkly. I shaved my legs, cut toe and fingernails and generally spruced up. I just needed some more oil to do the same for the bike. Yet again the room was festooned with damp camping equipment but I daren't get the tent out because it was sodden.

Fig. 52: the Plockton weather report

The B&B was part of an enterprise owned by Calum, Jane and daughter Fiona. Calum did seal spotting boat trips and they also had a gift shop, which amazingly had Sporks for sale. So I bought Spork number three which actually survived the journey and went home with me, to the delight of the grandchildren who eat porridge with it when they come to stay.

The Internet actually worked once Jane had switched it off and on again a couple of times, and I finally found a B&B with space for the following two nights, on the hill behind Plockton. So I was all set for a wee holiday.

day 24, Weds 22ⁿᵈ July: in and out of Plockton, 4.5 miles

some seal spotting

On impulse, I asked about the seal trips as I was leaving Mackenzie's, following a good night's sleep and a great breakfast. Jane phoned her husband and got the boat to wait for me and she even looked after the luggage and bike until I got back.

The Sula Mhor (it means big gannet apparently) started life in 1947 as a pleasure boat in Cornwall and Calum had been running boat trips for thirty years, with a money back guarantee if you did not see any seals. It was so much fun. His daughter Fiona was on board serving tea, Tunnock's caramel wafers and miniatures of whisky from the galley. Tunnock's caramel wafers, by the way, are a Scottish institution. They are made at a bakery in Uddingston near Glasgow, where I grew up. A shed outside our primary school used to sell big bags of Caramel Wafer off-cuts very cheaply and us kids ate them till we felt sick.

Children on board got to steer the boat and we had a good laugh, as well as seeing plenty of seals and Heron Island which was J M Barrie's inspiration for Peter Pan. Calum told everyone about Knit 1 Bike 1 as part of his commentary and refused all payment. I got some cracking seal photos and began crocheting seals over lunch as soon as I got back. The seal trips had a Trip Advisor Certificate of Excellence and I was not surprised.

Fig. 53: Calum on the Sula Mhor

Then I set off for Driseach B&B, where I had a bed for the next two nights with Joan and Iain. Their bungalow had amazing views of the Cuillins, which was very handy seeing as I was still crocheting them. They gave guests the run of their sitting room and kitchen along with a warm and friendly welcome.

I had a lovely big room and used their washing line to finally dry the tent out. There was a bit of drama going on in the background because one of their thirty cows was calving and could not be found. She was finally tracked down in the woods and the calf seemed to be dead but amazingly the vet was able to revive it.

Fig. 54: Plockton seals

They spent the next two days trying to keep track of the cow and find where she was hiding the calf, to make sure it got fed. So I hung out in their sitting room crocheting the Cuillins from the window and got the front part finished, before running out of yarn for the back. Lee posted more yarn up to the Highland Folk Museum but for now they were a project in abeyance.

day 25, Thursday 23rd July: a real day off – well almost... cycled 4.5 miles

Plockton continued to be sunny, whilst across the water Skye was shrouded in thick black clouds. The high winds continued on the islands and out at sea and Joan, Iain and I watched a couple of boats attempt to make it out of the harbour in the huge waves, although most chose to stay put. Joan declared that I was 'just like them' and even insisted I join them for some beans on toast for lunch. I was grateful because Plockton was an expensive place to eat. Then I hopped on the bike and whizzed down the hill into Plockton to explore. There was a Nepalese Bazaar in the village hall and I bought a woollen shawl and some wrist warmers, hoping they would make me warmer in the tent at night.

There was a wee community knitting shop in the village and Mary was sitting there knitting a cushion cover. The shop raised money for charity and was an offshoot of the knitting group which met in the library. The group had nineteen members – amazing given how tiny Plockton was. Mary was looking for a copy of Jean Greenhow's knitted nativity scene pattern book which I had at home, so I phoned Lee and he posted it to her.

Fig. 55: Joan and Iain at Driseach bed & breakfast

Further along the road was The Studio, where I bought some table mats produced by a local artist. The mats had drawings of birds printed onto them and were a wedding present for Liz and Graham, whom I had visited at Dalmally. I mailed them from the post office, which was really a glorified garden shed. You could reach it by walking across a causeway in the bay if the tide was out.

Fig. 56: Plockton post office

In the early afternoon I met three Australians, a couple and the woman's sister, down in the village. They were all wound up because there had been no one at home when they arrived at their B&B. By coincidence, they were booked in with Joan and Iain, so I told them the story of the missing calf and reassured them that most B&Bs would not expect guests until after 3pm anyway. They did seem to have a bit of an attitude problem, pronouncing that the B&B should have someone there all the time and sod the calf, basically. But hey, maybe it was just because they were away from home.

When I got back to Driseach though, there was a bit of a situation. They thought they had booked a double room and a single one - i.e. mine – but had actually booked the family room with a double bed and a single bed in it!

There were no other vacant rooms and Joan resolutely said it would do them no harm to share a room for the night and that they would just have to get on with it. They were rather abrasive and pushy and it almost seemed as if they were going to ask me to vacate the room for them.

My room was next to the bathroom and they spent most of the night waking me up by flushing the toilet. After it flushed for the fifth time, I wrote a notice on a piece of paper saying 'please do not flush the toilet' then leapt up and confronted the guy in his boxer shorts when it was flushed yet again. He announced that the loo 'had a poo in it' but I didn't care and just wanted some sleep.

day 26, Friday 24th July: Dingwall, cycled 9 miles – my kind of place

A quote: *'In knitting as in life there are usually two ways to go: the easy way and the hard way. Often we find out about the easy way only when we are three quarters of the way through with the hard way.' Ann Shayne and Kay Gardiner.*

The Kyle railway line was the next stage of the journey and I hopped – or rather scrambled – aboard at Plockton Station. The station buildings were now holiday cottages and there was a notice on the platform asking people to be quiet whilst waiting for the train. The old-style platform was almost two feet lower than the train and there was also a wide horizontal gap. There was a wee stool on the platform for passengers to use when boarding, but it was not much use with the bike. It was the worst gap yet and I got stuck half way yet again. I just had to wait there, arms extended with the bike half on and half off until the conductor helped.

A railway enthusiast went up and down the train telling people about the historic Kyle railway line. He said there had been a sea eagle following the train for the last few days, although it did not make an appearance for us. I got a certificate to say Knit 1 Bike 1 had travelled on the line though. A Chinese guy sitting opposite was also a cyclist and although he spoke no English other than the words 'China' and 'Inverness' we managed quite well with sign language and gestures. He was cycling either round the world or round Scotland - I could not work out which - and had fallen off his bike and skinned his knuckles. He had a good look at my map as his was nothing more than a pen drawing on the back of a menu. It was surprisingly accurate though and he was reassured.

I hopped off the train at Garve and cycled the remaining nine miles to Dingwall, where there were some charity shops, a Lidl supermarket, a cafe or two and even a bike shop. What was really a small Highland town seemed like quite a metropolis. The Camping and Caravanning Club site was right in the centre, walking distance from the shops. It was satisfying to get the Club's over 55s discount and pay only £7.90 a night.

Fig. 57: Chinese cyclist on the train to Inverness

Dingwall and the Audax

The purpose of being in Dingwall was to visit the National Cycle Audax, which was due to set off from there the following afternoon. The cyclists would cover two hundred and fifty miles/four hundred kilometres in twenty seven hours or less, and organisers Denise and Steve had invited me to join them for breakfast when the riders came back on Sunday.

As well as being a cyclist, Denise was a keen knitter and member of the Highland Guild of Weavers, Spinners and Dyers. We had connected via Facebook and she and Steve had given invaluable advice about routes in the area.

Lots of the riders were camping at the site and there was a bit of a carnival atmosphere. Emma and her hubby were in the next tent and made me cups of tea on their stove. They were real adventurers and had done things like kayak around Alaska and get marooned in a bay hundreds of miles from anyone, trapped by icebergs. A guy camping on the other side had already cycled from Newcastle, was doing the 250 miles/400km Audax overnight and then cycling home again ready for work on Monday. And I had hopped on the train and cycled nine miles from Garve.

People in the checkout queue at Lidl all joined in the discussion on where I should eat that evening and the unanimous verdict was the Thai cafe round the corner. The food was wonderful, the place quirky and the bill only £6.90.

Fig. 58: the folded Brompton in the tent at Dingwall

For the first time having now travelled further east, there were no midges and I finally realised the Knit 1 Bike 1 fantasy of being able to sit in the doorway of the tent and knit. There was torrential rain from 6pm onwards but it was warm and with the tent door open I could actually see out instead of being sealed inside. I slept well despite the continuing downpour and woke to find it was so wet that worms had crawled up the inside of the flysheet and were plopping down onto the inner tent. The Brompton, by the way, fitted snugly into the doorway in this smallest of small tents.

Fig. 59: knitted worms and other creatures

day 27, Saturday 25th July: a day in Dingwall

It was fun chatting to the various Audax riders in the morning and Aiden offered me a ride on his tandem trike. His riding partner Judith was staying in a hotel, wise woman.

We hurtled through Dingwall on the tandem, to visit the cash machine and buy a macaroni pie as extra rations for Aiden on the Audax. It was weird having no control and not being able to see where we were going. I had hiking boots on and could not 'clip on' to the cleats on the tiny metal pedals, so just prayed my feet would not slip off.

Because it was a trike you had to lean the opposite way to normal when going round corners and Aiden actually got out of the saddle and hung over the side like you would in a sailing dinghy. He probably had to, to counteract my tendency to lean the wrong way, mind you.

Then I cycled rather more slowly to the start of the Audax via the local bike shop, where the chain got oiled at last. The riders set off in batches of twenty. They were a laid back bunch, with no one the slightest bit bothered if they started a bit later than someone else. One guy meandered up at the end, wondering how he had managed to be late to the start, because he had been there ages.

There were all kinds of bikes including several two-wheeled tandems and the tandem trike I had ridden on. The majority of riders would never see forty five again and a good number were ten or twenty years older than that. I had read that if you cycled eighty miles a week your body age would be twenty years less than your actual age. This lot were younger than their kids then.

Fig. 60: the tandem trike with Aiden

food in the Highlands

Dingwall was cheaper than the trendy places like Plockton and I loved it. I had missed the old-style Scottish pubs, which no longer existed in much of the Highlands. With their swirly patterned carpets, beaten copper tables and Artex walls, you used to be able to sit in a gloomy corner all day nursing half a pint of fizzy water and no one bothered you.

Now they were trendy restaurants packed with tourists. The food looked pretty but you never quite got enough to eat, even though it cost £25 a head. They wanted you in and out in ninety minutes and you had to book. The worst part was that the only place left to sit and have a drink was perched at the bar on a high stool – not much good for knitting, but understandable of course, if you are a hotelier trying to make a living.

The cafes were the same. Gone were the wood-chip papered walls and red gloss-paint. You could no longer get a baked potato and coleslaw with a bit of Iceberg lettuce and slice of tinned pineapple on the side for 3.50. Lunch cost £15 and had pine nuts on it. In other words, my daily food bill was sometimes £40 when it was too midgy or cold to have a picnic. On other days it could be £5 if there was a local Co-op and the weather was better.

In Dingwall, I finally sussed it. Not that Dingwall *was* particularly trendy, thank goodness. Community cafes were the answer but you had to ask around and would never find them on your own. I asked someone who was setting up a sea pollution display in a gazebo outside the museum and she directed me to go to The Greenhouse Community cafe. That is when I finally got it and I knew to look for community cafes from then on.

Fig. 61: the Audax sets off

She directed me through the charity shop and up the stairs at the back to the cafe. It served tea and when I arrived the volunteer staff went out and bought some cakes, asking for a £2 donation. They loaned me a community laptop and the cafe provided wifi and a place to sit for as long as I wanted. You could even have brought your own sandwiches with you and nobody would mind.

The only other customer was an African drumming tutor, who came in to use a laptop once a week because he had a computer-free home. An interesting concept, because he did not spend an hour a day answering emails and another hour on Facebook like I did at home. When he used the computer, he had to leave his own front door and had social contact in the process.

A few others had drifted in by mid-morning and all were locals. I got the photos backed up and was able to write in comfort. It was raining heavily outside again and I felt very lucky to be indoors – there really was not much to do in a small tent in the cold and wet other than stay in the sleeping bag and read or knit. Because I did not have a chair, even that got to be hard work after a while.

Fig. 62: Denise and Steve, Audax organisers

In the afternoon there was a band playing there as part of the local sea pollution awareness festival. I went back to the cafe to hear them but it was very crowded and in the end I gave up. I had chatted to the band earlier on and they were doing a challenge that involved touring round Scotland and playing at as many small venues as possible.

day 28, Sunday 26th July: Dingwall to Inverness, 15 miles

The day's greatest challenge was packing the bike bags. All the food from Lidl had to be squeezed in somehow and the tent was soaking wet, on the inside and outside of the fly sheet. The whole lot was one soggy mess by the time it was rolled up, not helped by the protective groundsheet that went underneath the tent. This was a piece cut from an old tent that I remembered growing up with and despite re-proofing was still not waterproof. It had originally belonged to my father and I believe it was made from an old wartime parachute – what was I thinking?

The water seeped through, then sat between it and the tent floor, causing a puddle in the rear rucksack when it was packed away. The tent and groundsheet were permanently stuck together whenever the ground had been damp overnight, (which was always) and could not be separated until it was possible to dry everything out. It also made the tent floor cold to the touch. I had been telling myself that the old groundsheet did its job nevertheless, as it protected the tent bottom from stones - but it was time to get a new one.

Then I headed off to Dingwall Community Centre to meet up with Denise and Steve and join the Audax for breakfast, wearing the Knit 1 Bike 1 crocheted tabard. For once the tabard was actually useful as it meant I did not have to keep explaining that I had *not* just finished the Audax. There was a motley collection of sweaty riders back already, sitting round a table eating a mixture of egg and bacon rolls, soup and left over trifle. Some of them were nodding off at the table and all were cramming in as much food as possible. There was no sign of Aiden and Judith on the tandem trike, but one of the two wheeled tandems was back, which was really good going, as tandems are harder work than a regular bicycle.

Denise had been up all night but she was determined to find time to chat and we sat knitting together in a quiet room upstairs. She was knitting a very complicated sock with a separate panel up the front that had to be grafted on afterwards. I finally set off for Inverness at 11.45 full of bacon and egg and had a lovely fifteen mile cycle along Sustrans Route One, which went all the way there.

On arriving at Inverness, there was the usual puddle in the bottom of the rucksack caused by the tent. Thankfully the clothes were in plastic bags and everything stayed dry. Something much larger than a midge had bitten me on the rear and I took an antihistamine, as the resultant lump was already half an inch/1.25cm across. Bught caravan site was huge and right in the centre of Inverness. The best thing of all was that it had great facilities and a separate, vehicle-free camping field for backpackers and cyclists. Being in the town, the field was surrounded by suburbia. I was camped on one side of a chain link fence with my knickers hung on it to dry, whilst on the other side a bowling match was taking place.

The site had an internet 'cafe', which was a Portacabin with a snack machine, space to sit, wifi, somewhere to charge phones and chat. There was much swapping of stories and I had a lovely chat with a couple of Polish cyclists who had bailed out of Skye at the same time as me due to the weather.

They had carried a full sized laptop all the way from Poland and after three weeks, this was the first place that had usable, functioning wifi. A guy in his fifties lived on Fair Isle and had cycled all the way from there on a mountain bike with those fat, jumbo knobbly tyres, which must have been really hard work.

There was a mobile hotel from overseas on the site, consisting of a huge trailer pulled by a lorry. It had three storeys of individual sleeping pods each with its own little window. The people travelled by a coach during the day and slept in the trailer at night. The pods looked rather like coffins and it would not be funny if you ended up being surrounded by snoring fellow guests on all sides.

A food van visited the site morning and evening which meant a cheap dinner. Busy sites like this one, with amenities and situated in towns definitely made for the best Knit 1 Bike 1 camping. The complete opposite to the quiet, secluded ones we usually favoured when camping with a car. The camping field had about forty tents in it but because everyone was travelling on foot or by bike we all went to bed early and there was complete silence by 10pm.

Fig. 63: the Rollende Camping Hotel at Inverness

day 29, Monday 27th July: Inverness to Aviemore by train, cycled 5 miles

After another chilly night wearing all the clothes I had with me, it was time to buy a warmer sleeping bag. Why had I not thought to do so before - I could have got one in Fort William. Inverness was large and after wandering around for half an hour without finding an outdoor shop, I took an earlier train, planning to shop for one in Aviemore instead.

Aviemore was a place I knew and loved. It was familiar and had lots of cafes and outdoor shops. Getting there would also mean I had travelled up Scotland as far as I was going, cycled across from west to east and would be going south from then on - a real milestone.

Having tried various sleeping bags to make sure they would fit in the bike bag, I settled on a three season down bag. For good measure, several dri bags for clothes and the phone, map etc. and a very expensive groundsheet to go underneath the tent were added to the pile.

I left the shop feeling like a load had been lifted off my shoulders, realising I had been in survival mode for the last few days. The old sleeping bag was deposited in a charity shop which was a shame as there was nothing wrong with it but there was no way of carrying both. I just did not have the resources to work out how to post it home.

No wonder it was hard to be creative with the knitting and crochet, it had taken so much energy just to stay warm and cheerful. So feeling perky, I decided to stay an extra night in Aviemore and dropped into the local library to arrange a visit to their Knit 'n' Natter group the following evening.

I popped into the quirky Skiing Doo for dinner telling them about Knit 1 Bike 1. They presented me with a huge slap-up meal and refused all payment.

Then I spent a delicious, warm and cosy night in the sleeping bag, wearing nothing more than a tee shirt. I still had not done any crocheting or knitting, but resolved to post the half-knitted socks home as they were causing too much of a distraction.

day 30, Tuesday 28th July: Rothiemurchus campsite to Aviemore and back, 8 miles

It was a brisk cycle into Aviemore first thing to visit the Active Cafaidh. It was a cafe above an outdoor shop, and along with an outdoor activities business was owned by Roy and Sophia. It turned out they used to live in Cumnock a few miles away from home and we even knew them vaguely. The cafe was run by their niece Carrie-Anne and offered free porridge with any cafe purchase before 10am -who could resist? I added a cooked breakfast for good measure.

Fig. 64: the Active Cafaidh, Aviemore

a call from Radio Scotland

I was just feeling smug about being so well organised and having an extra night in Aviemore, when The Kaye Adams Show from Radio Scotland phoned. They wanted to do a live interview the following morning, which would mean a very early start in order to reach Newtonmore before the interview.

This was a sorting things out and a yarn day though and I decided to continue with both that and with the planned visit to the Knit 'N' Natter in Aviemore Library. What a library it was too, open seven days a week and until 10pm on week days. Meanwhile, at home East Ayrshire Council were closing my local library and several others.

Fig. 65: a hedgehog knitted by a member of Aviemore Knitting Group (pattern by King Cole)

Aviemore Knit 'N' Natter group

It was so nice to just knit and well, natter with the library group that evening and the mad woman on a bicycle was made very welcome. I crocheted a whole seal which would be part of a group of them on a rock just like the ones at Plockton. One member had knitted a hedgehog and another was working on poppies for Remembrance Day, so I bought one to add to the Knit 1 Bike 1 exhibition. Then I cycled back to the campsite and went straight to bed, planning an early start in the morning.

a rather average campsite

The Rothiemurchus campsite near Aviemore was the second most expensive of the whole trip. The most expensive was at Blair Atholl a couple of days later. Whereas Blair Atholl was a wonderful site and worth the money, Rothiemurchus did not feel quite so welcoming to campers.

Rothiemurchus put their tents in a public area of the woods with a footpath going through it, outside the main campsite. Dog walkers and mountain bikers went past the higher up section all the time and midges congregated in the shade of the trees. There was a lower section which was quieter but prone to being flooded by the river and the warden said it was best avoided.

There were notices telling campers not to bail out into the toilet block or laundry if they were flooded out, but just to disappear and not bother anyone basically. The toilets, showers and dishwashing area themselves were fine and brand new, but they consisted of unisex large cubicles, each including a loo and shower. This meant long queues at peak times.

There were notices saying you were not allowed to do laundry anywhere other than in the washing machines ten minutes walk away on the main site. There were also notices listing a number of other things you were not allowed to do.

The signs created a grumpy atmosphere and it felt as if they wanted the revenue from the tents but not the bother. The laundry was £4 minimum for a basic wash and dry, there was no laundry sink that you could wash a few things out in and nowhere to hang clothes out to dry, so you had to use the tumble dryer. Just my opinion of course – I spoke to a caravanner staying in the main field and he loved it.

day 31, Wednesday 29ᵗʰ July: Rothiemurchus to Newtonmore, 21 miles

A month today since the journey began and it felt like a year. Would I ever be home again, and how strange would it be getting back to normal life? I was up at six and on the road by 7.40 though, feeling very pleased with myself. Then a brisk cycle to the campsite at Newtonmore, to get there in good time for the Radio Scotland interview. The site owner must have felt sorry for me because she gave me 20p for a free shower. In contrast to Rothiemurchus, this site was also the cheapest at £4 a night.

As luck would have it, the campsite had good mobile reception and a plug socket in the laundry room where I could charge the phone up. The interview took place with me sitting on a bench outside the loo block and luckily it was quiet. Two minutes after it finished a tanker arrived and started to pump out the septic tank. Phew – that was a close one!

Fig. 66: Newtonmore, location of the Kaye Adams Show interview

workshop number 9: the Highland Folk Museum

The afternoon's knitting workshop was at the Highland Folk Museum. The museum was a free open air venue with buildings and activities over a wide area and a tractor and trailer to take people to different parts of the site. There was everything from a 17ᵗʰ century settlement to a 1950s school house and lots going on, such as Highland life in the 17ᵗʰ Century demonstrations and people in costume to tell you about the different exhibits. A pretend teacher in the reconstructed primary school was giving everyone lessons to do and demonstrated the old fashioned 'belt' used to hit children in schools in the past. The belt was unique to Scotland, with the rest of the UK using a cane to hit *their* children with.

Fig. 67: teacher demonstrates the belt at the Folk Museum

The stranded knitting workshop took place in a re-located 1940s corrugated iron church and the cleaner who worked at the museum came along. I thought that was going to be it but a teenager and her dad arrived because they had heard the Radio Scotland interview. Several other people joined in just because they had come to see the church including another teenager who was very keen.

The campsite was transformed when I got back there, as people were arriving for the weekend's Highland games, due to take place in a field opposite. The caravans were packed in, children were practising their Highland dance routine and two Labradoodles were racing round in circles. The group of older men who kept their caravans on the site all-year-round were clearly enjoying the entertainment and the bench outside the shower block was crowded.

There was an old fashioned truckstop-cum-diner opposite the site and that looked like a good venue for breakfast the following day.

There were lots of trucks parked outside it - usually a sign of good value food. I called in to check what time they began serving breakfast and they apologised for not being open until 5.30am – plenty early enough for me and then some. There was an extensive menu, showers and even knitted jumpers for sale.

Fig. 68: church at the Folk Museum, venue for workshop no. 9

day 32, Thurs 30th July: Newtonmore to Blair Atholl, 34 miles

The spiffy new sleeping bag was leaking down everywhere. It was seeping out through the fabric itself and there was not a tear or a break in the stitching anywhere. It got in my eyes and mouth, stuck to clothes and coated the floor of the tent. You know that thing where all your energy goes into being solution-focused and positive and then it does not work out and you have just got nothing left? Well for a few minutes, this sleeping bag was that. But hey, it had still kept me warm and would do until I got to Dundee and could take it back to another branch of the same shop. It had not rained the previous night (!) and the new ground sheet underneath the tent was a success. There was no big puddle underneath and the tent floor was now warm instead of cold to the touch. What is more, I would be in Perth and Kinross by the afternoon. *And* I had now camped for six nights in a row, which was a lifetime record.

There had been fourteen camping nights on the trip so far. I now needed to do a lot more camping to be ahead financially, having bought the sleeping bag and groundsheet. The camping was worthwhile in other ways though and the tent gave me my own space. Having proved I could still enjoy it, I was also determined to camp again, so the equipment would not be wasted.

Fig. 69: a trucker's breakfast

Hubby was bringing the caravan to Dunkeld so I would see him the following day *and* get to sleep in our wee caravan. Better than the tent, but how I craved another hot bath, a comfy sofa and central heating. Yes, it really was cold enough to crave central heating in July.

Fig. 70: the top of Drumochter Pass

Drumochter Pass

The day's route included going over the Drumochter Pass. There were dire warnings at the start of the cycleway, saying bad weather could come down suddenly, there was nowhere to get food and it was a 395m summit. Oh crumbs! I checked the map but there was no other route except the busy A9. Then common sense clicked in. The cycleway goes along the side of the A9 for most of the way anyway. I had just had a cake stop and had food, water, a tent and super warm sleeping bag with me - and it was July.

Fig. 71: a Sustrans bench made out of skis

The whole thing turned out to be a very gentle climb then a blissful downhill and flat ride all the way to Blair Atholl. I still paused at the top though and a family from London took a photo. Halfway along the route was a bench made by Sustrans volunteers out of old skis, a reminder of what the weather could be like there at other times of the year.

The Blair Atholl campsite had a couple of Highland cows which helpfully posed for photos outside the gate and the site itself had all mod cons. At £15 a night this was the most expensive camp of the trip, but for a cyclist it was worth every penny. There were comfy sofas and a tea machine in reception which I monopolised for several hours, sitting there in comfort whilst working on some more crocheted seals. There was also a games room which stayed open until 10pm, so there was a warm comfy place to crochet and knit all evening. It did feel a bit strange hanging out with the teenagers but they soon got used to me being there.

There were few distractions on a trip like this and it had stripped away my defences. With no 'busyness' to hide behind, emotions were much nearer the surface. It would not do to get mired in one's thoughts, e.g. how far there was still to cycle, being tired, being alone... so distraction and keeping busy were important. I reflected on how easy it had become to do what the meditation class back home suggested - just noticing the emotions and letting them pass, whilst being in the moment. I was finally able to do it.

Fig. 72: Highland cattle at Blair Atholl

day 33, Fri 31st July: Blair Atholl to Dunkeld and getting lost, 26 miles

What was supposed to be a nineteen-mile cycle ended up being a whole lot more due to a wrong turning. This was the third day of cycling in a row and the previous day's ride had been the longest of the trip so far.

I did not feel especially tired in the morning but had been disturbed by two rather tipsy young men coming back to their tent late the night before. One of them had a loud phone conversation with his girlfriend that went on for some time. Apparently I could have phoned security and the site had strict rules about noise but eventually I called out to the guys to please be quiet and it worked, thank goodness.

As this was supposed to be an easy day and mostly downhill, I did not set off until 11am. Lee was setting off from Ayrshire at about the same time and we were both aiming to reach the caravan site at Dunkeld by late afternoon. I set off grand style but stopped to investigate an artisan bakery-cum-cafe just down the road from the site. Having had only oatcakes and fruit for breakfast, it seemed a good idea to stock up before cycling any further and the bakery had a whole range of good stuff.

After Killiecrankie the route was actually very hilly, far more so than Drumochter pass, and I was glad of the egg roll and cake from the bakers. The road finally levelled out after several miles, only to become steep again on leaving Pitlochry. Then I turned right instead of left, despite a Sustrans Route 77 sign. I only guessed several miles later, because two young men on mountain bikes with huge rucksacks had been behind me doing the same route and did not appear when I stopped for a break.

Then the minor road came out onto the A9 just half a mile from where I needed to go but it was too busy to get across. Route 77 sent me on a cycle path beside the A9 going back up towards Inverness and Aviemore. Having gone wrong once already and being too knackered to do even more extra miles, I was super-careful and doubled back to check the signs again. There was a post with two footpath signs on it, both saying 'Dunkeld 2¼ miles and pointing in opposite directions!

Fig. 73: Dunkeld, which way?

I found out later it was a circular walk but at the time, too tired to even think straight, I finally followed route 77 towards Aviemore regardless. It soon turned back on itself and continued to Dunkeld along the very muddy circular footpath, meaning I had to push the bike. Having emerged into Dunkeld disorientated and with no idea which way to go, I phoned Lee for directions. Coming to an unexpected junction I tried to phone again, only to find that the phone had a cracked screen and would not work at all. I took a guess and turned right, soon realising it was the right road for the campsite.

Fig. 74: Janet and Lee rendevouz at Dunkeld

At the site, neighbouring campers reported that Lee had gone out with his camera to intercept me, thinking I was coming from the other direction. He was phoning but the call would not pick up on the broken phone, so I borrowed someone else's phone to ring him before he called out a search party.

We spent a lovely couple of hours catching up and eating dinner before heading off to see dear friends Margaret and Andrew of Appletree Man nursery in nearby Bankfoot, where they produce and sell organic fruit trees and herbs from their home. And Lee was able to collect the tea bush to take home with him.

Margaret and Andrew's sofa was wonderful and although we were only there for the evening they offered me a bath. I spent a good half hour in the hot water before joining the others for a lovely evening of catching up, drinking beer and eating nibbles. Margaret was very complimentary about the crocheted seals (there were now two) and had booked a place on the following day's workshop at the Birnam Institute.

day 34, Sat 1st Aug: getting things sorted out, cycled 4 miles

I had been looking forward to some time off and imagined relaxing and eating would be the main activities during this wee break. Lee had brought the laptop though and there were several emails and phone calls about workshops that needed dealing with. We also had to go into Dundee to change the sleeping bag and buy a new mobile phone. I had to compile a power point presentation for Monday's talk in Dundee and the photos needed backing up again. The blog was out of date because Blogger had compatibility issues with the broken phone and had not let me upload photographs.

Then there were a host of small things, like straightening tent pegs, polishing the boots and cleaning and oiling the bike. And of course writing, crocheting and knitting and delivering a workshop at the Birnam Institute. So actually no days off for me, and Lee mucked in to help as much as possible. It was all good fun though and I do love that kind of work-play mix, which is so much a part of life as a textile artist. At home I would often roll out of bed in pyjamas and cross the hall straight into the studio, only realising at lunch time that I was still not dressed. So now I was sitting up in bed in the caravan and working on a power point presentation. Not much had changed really.

Fig. 75: Desperate Dan

So in the true spirit of Knit 1 Bike 1, we had fun in Dundee whilst doing what we had to do, taking both Bromptons with us in Lee's van. Having parked in a housing estate on the outskirts, we had a very cheap lunch of mince and tatties in a local cafe before cycling into the town centre. Lee took a picture of me under the Desperate Dan statue, which commemorates the Beano and Dandy comics produced in the city for many years.

At midnight, I had been on the road for just over 34½ days and the journey would be half way through. I was really chuffed and far more confident that I would actually make it all the way. Being in the caravan with Lee was to make it harder to gird my loins and set off again the following day though. There was no excitement and adrenalin this time, like there had been on day one.

Fig. 76: penguin sculptures looking smart

day 35, Sun 2nd Aug: the Birnam Institute, cycled 2 miles

workshop number 10

After a lot of meandering on the first part of the trip up the West Coast, I was now covering a lot more ground and it seemed no time at all since Aviemore. I had cycled eighty one miles in three days to reach Dunkeld, with no adverse effects. Twenty miles mostly felt like a walk in the park, yet I had struggled a little to cycle a similar distance two weeks before setting off. Birnam and Dunkeld are two tiny Perthshire villages that run into one another. The Birnam Institute was in Beatrix Potter country and had a permanent exhibition of her work and life. Beatrix, who wrote the famous 'Peter Rabbit' children's stories, holidayed in the area with her family when she was aged 5 to 16, only holidaying in the Lake district, where her connection is better known, later on.

Fig. 77: the Birnam Institute

More notable for me though, the Institute had a great exhibition and workshop space, theatre productions and a cafe. Arts team member Jan had organised the workshop there and kept us supplied with hot drinks, scones and Eton Mess. She was helpful and friendly, encouraging several people to come and have a look what we were doing. We laid out some of the Knit 1 Bike 1 art work so that people could see it and I took advantage of the room's excellent lighting to photograph it.

Fig. 78: Margaret learns to do stranded knitting

In the evening, Lee and I went out for dinner with Margaret and Andrew. They had managed to find a pub that served stovies because I wanted some good plain cooking after all those fancy pub meals. For those who do not know, stovies is a Scottish dish consisting of mashed potato and minced beef or lamb all mixed in together. It looks terrible and tastes divine.

day 36, Monday 3ʳᵈ Aug: Dunkeld to Dundee, 29 miles

Twenty nine miles and delivering a workshop the same evening was a bit of a rush. I had done a similar thing on Mull though and only hoped there was time for a shower and some dinner beforehand. It was a mostly flat route and the sun came out at Coupar Angus, the half way point. Whilst I was sitting on a bench eating lunch, Ben from the Coupar Angus Cycling Hub came over and introduced himself. His family lived not far from us so we had a good chat about Ayrshire and he showed me the Cycling Hub headquarters. The Hub encouraged people to use cycling as an alternative to some car trips and whilst I was there a family of four came in, looking for advice on buying bicycles.

Fig. 79: Knit 1 Bike 1 artwork

They had an assortment of bikes for hire, including two Bromptons and were funded by the climate change fund. Bromptons are of course ideal for short trips and commuting (as well as for cycling round Scotland on!) because you can easily take one with you in the car, on the train or even the bus.

"A to B" magazine, which is especially for those of us with folding bikes, makes the point that there is often a "missing link" when using public transport. This is a part of the journey that takes ages because the transport or timetables do not connect well - and that's when you hop on the Brompton. It was great to come across a cycle project in Scotland that had not only heard of Bromptons but had a couple of them available.

A textile project had taken up residence in one of the Hub's spare rooms and members had covered a children's bike and tricycle in knitting. The trike even had a boot full of knitted vegetables. Although Ben tried phoning, there was no one from the textile project available to meet up - if only I had known about them in advance. His colleague was just setting off to meet up with some kids in the park. He was riding on the project's ice cream trike, complete with an insulated box full of ice cream on the front, so he would no doubt be popular.

Fig. 80: Ben from Coupar Angus Cycling Hub

workshop No 11: Fluph yarn shop

After lunch I cycled on to meet Leona, the owner of Fluph yarn shop in Dundee. Leona was hosting the evening's talk, feeding me and providing a bed for the night. We had corresponded by e mail but never met so I could not wait to see her.

Fig. 81: the tricycle covered in knitting

Leona and Mark lived on the second floor of a traditional sandstone Dundee tenement block, typical of those found in many Scottish cities. The flats were built around central drying greens with a huge central pole in the middle, the height of the three storey building. This had pulleys at each level with a washing line going to every flat. The pole on Leona's back green was still operational and she used it regularly, leaning out of the window to peg the washing on it then using the pulley system to haul it in again when it was dry.

Fluph, like many yarn shops, was out of the main drag and a real find. Fourteen knitters came to the 'talk and knit' and the slide show seemed to go down well. There was lots of cake, including some dairy-free with meringue, which was irresistible. There were some amazing knitting projects on the go too, and knitters of every level from near beginners to experts, all of whom made me welcome.

Fig. 82: Leona's washing dries on the pulley system

day 37, Tuesday 4th August: Dundee to Newburgh, 17.5 miles

How could you cycle round Scotland alone for sixty nine days and not notice that you were fit and strong? I could camp in all weather and manage on my own, albeit with the support and help of family and friends, and was becoming more confident daily. I had learned to ask others for help and to notice what was around, like the Buzz project bus near Fort William. Setting off in the mornings was still a slow business, but it was fun to potter in the cafes and there was no one to please but myself. So I had ditched the "rule" that you are supposed to set off early, and decided that stopping at the first cafe was just fine.

This started out as a crazy project but friends and family said things like 'go for it' and 'we are proud of you'. Because of their support, and as the following on social media grew, it seemed less crazy and more real. The Facebook following was a significant support on the journey and several people made a point of sending regular messages whilst I was en route, which made an incredible difference. Having cycled over four hundred miles and got past the halfway point on the sixty nine day trip, I was not going to crawl home embarrassed even if something prevented me from finishing the whole thing. The crochet and knitting were working out, although finishing things was still a challenge. The pieces were not fussy or perfect, for example the seals had no eyes, but they had a really good seal shape and would look effective on a crocheted rock out at sea.

Fig. 83: the talk at Fluph Yarn shop

Today's ride was a challenging, hilly, seventeen miles in a strong head wind but maybe it was harder because of a longish cycle the day before. Having left Leona's at 10.20, I stopped at a cafe in Dundee for a coffee to wait out the heavy rain, then stopped at another one on the far side of the Tay bridge having smelled bacon. So by 12.00 I had cycled two miles, stopped at two cafes and just made it across the Tay bridge. Who cared? The bacon roll was a mistake though as it made me thirsty, and the sun came out soon afterwards. With five miles still to go, the water bottle was nearly empty and it was with relief that I remembered the cucumber Leona had given me. It saved the day and provided enough hydration to get me to Newburgh.

The Newburgh Inn was pretty much the only place to stay in the town and there were no campsites. It did not do food but the landlord offered to heat up a microwave meal if I bought one from the Coop. He even set me up with a plate and knife and fork in the bar. It was great because it was so much cheaper than a meal out and I added a head of lettuce, another cucumber and some bananas for good measure.

Colourful felt studio Little Twist was located just behind the main street in Newburgh and I paid a visit to Laura there, who makes felt and sells supplies to other felt makers. It was lovely to catch up and see her work.

Fig. 84: the Tay Bridge

day 38, Wednesday 5th August: Newburgh to Kinross, 17 miles

A third day of cycling in a row and I was tired – but only month to go. It was tempting to stay another night in Newburgh, but I needed to get to Kinross for the following day's workshop. Setting off reluctantly, I cycled the first mile only to find the room key in my pocket and had to go back again, finally getting going for real at 10.20.

Fig. 85: Laura at Little Twist Felt Studio

There were only another twelve miles to go and all day to cycle to Kinross so I decided to go with the flow rather than push on. There really was not much choice as I had little energy and just wanted a nap, so I stopped at Abernethy.

Having tried without success to find out if there was anything left of the Abernethy biscuit factory, I took some pictures of Abernethy tower, an ideal crochet subject. It had a neck manacle thing on the side of it, which someone on Facebook told me is called a 'joug' and was used as a punishment, like stocks.

The tearoom opposite had the key if you wanted to climb the tower but with stiff knees and not much energy, tea and cake was more inviting. Setting off again with renewed vigour I trundled up long, slow climbs without much trouble, so it was a good day's cycling after all – albeit with frequent rest stops.

Fig. 86: Abernethy Tower

Despite having phoned to confirm several times and telling the campsite that I was on a bike with a tent, there were no toilets or other facilities on the site, which they had not thought to mention. It was just an empty field with electric hook ups. The woman in the house at the end of the site just said 'no' when I enquired about facilities then shut the door! No wonder the place was deserted.

A nearby bed and breakfast had no room but directed me to another campsite – there were several in the area - and after pitching up I cycled into Kinross to find Skeins & Bobbins, the venue for the following day's workshop. The guy on the campsite was, if anything, a little over helpful when he found out I was alone, and I made a point of being matter of fact in discussion with him, then pitched the tent and thought no more about it.

Morag's shop had been open for only three months, although she and her sister had sold things via craft fairs for a while. She was loving it and did lots of childrens knitting lessons at the shop, which were a real hit. A friendly pub let me charge the phone up whilst eating dinner, something that was a challenge on most campsites, unless you wanted to spend the evening sitting beside a plug socket in the laundry block.

Fig. 87: neck joug, Abernethy Tower

day 39, Thursday 6ᵗʰ Aug: cycled 4 miles

campsite challenges

A lovely sunny morning and it looked like there would be a second mild and pleasant night's camping to come, but it was not to be. Just before noon, I went to the ladies loo block and the over-friendly campsite guy came in behind me, saying he needed to mop the floor. He took up the resident mop that lived outside the shower cubicles and gave it a token going over, then leaned against the wall and proceed to chat whilst I was brushing my teeth! What to do, walk out, or ignore him? I carried on brushing and he eventually left, saying "right then, if that's how it is" in a rather offended voice.

workshop number 12

Feeling rather creeped out by the whole thing, I cycled into Kinross for the workshop at Skeins & Bobbins and told Morag about it, just in case there were any further problems. She looked me in the eye and stated the obvious. If there was any concern at all, which there was because otherwise why mention it, I needed to move from the site. What if the silly bloke came to the tent at night for another 'chat'?

Lee said the same thing when I phoned home and booked me a B&B. He was straightforward about life being just too short to put up with stuff like that. The whole incident was strange rather than scary but especially on a solo trip it was better not to get into situations in the first place. Yet again, the support had been there, not just from Lee but from Morag as well.

Fig. 88: Morag and her sister at Skeins & Bobbins

So it was back to the campsite after the workshop to pack up the tent, then back into Kinross yet again to unpack at the B&B and have dinner with Morag. She gave me a beautiful hank of laceweight yarn and two egg cups with dinky wee knitted bunny egg cosies on them. She also insisted on paying for the meal. The rest of the evening was spent finishing the crocheted profile of the Cuillins and I photographed it placed on the shelf above the wash basin in the bedroom. It got lots of "likes" on Facebook.

The room had a shared bathroom. I spent a restless night and was wary of who might be around during a nocturnal trip to the loo, not something that would have usually bothered me at all. The campsite incident was the only unpleasant encounter of the whole trip though, apart from a couple of occasions when an irate motorist shouted out of a car window.

day 40, Friday 7th August: Kinross to Stirling, 26 miles

A day off from cycling had made a difference and I set off at 10am far more energetic. Major work was taking place in the centre of Kinross and the whole high street was closed, with diversion signs everywhere. I cycled round in circles for a while before finally finding the A811, but once on it, the going was easy and the traffic light. It was sunny and hot so I stopped at a pub in Fishcross for a cold drink just in case there was nothing further on. A couple of miles later was Powfoot Milk Bar though, with mountains of cakes and a trip down memory lane. It had been there since the 1960s and reminded me of the old Ayrshire milk bars. I had some tea but unfortunately got into a tea-pee cycle and had to go in third cafe for a loo stop later on, which of course meant buying yet another cup of tea.

Fig. 89: cakes at Powfoot Milk Bar

The road was closed a few miles after Powfoot with a diversion in place. These can be a particular problem when cycling, as you never know how many miles the diversion is going to be, so with fingers crossed I set off. My luck was in, and half a mile later the road emerged directly opposite the Sustrans cycle route into Stirling, so the rest of the trip was on quiet lanes or off-road - after a pause at cafe number three in Alva. The fourth tea stop of the day was in Stirling itself and I ate a late packed lunch on a bench before getting a cuppa and piece of cake to finish it off. There were people practising on pipes and drums in the parks and the sound filled the air. It was because of a piping competition of course but made me chuckle and imagine foreign tourists thinking that maybe Scots just went to the park to play the pipes on a sunny day.

Stirling is bike friendly and there was a network of tunnels under the roads in the town centre. The local Bike Hub project was holding a cycling festival with all sorts of events over the following couple of days. I cycled through a city centre tunnel and a cycle counter told me I was the 307th cyclist to go through that day.

Mary and John had generously offered to put me up for the night even though we had never met and they had only returned from their holiday earlier the same day. Mary crocheted unique and quirky things for friends, such as a pair of binoculars and some birds for a retiring colleague, so it was lovely to see her work.

After a warm welcome and lots of delicious food I realised how tired I was. We watched the Great British Bake Off on TV and I crocheted another seal at the same time, then slept so soundly I did not wake up until 8.45am, to find everyone else had been up for ages. I was definitely getting the hang of sleeping away from home.

days 41 & 42, Saturday 9th/ Sunday 10th August: Stirling to Paisley, cycled 9.5 miles

It was hard to say goodbye, realising that like so many of the generous people encountered on this trip I may never see Mary, John and their daughter again. It was strange to connect, then disconnect and move on, like being in a bubble and somewhat removed from normal life going on all around. The miles were disappearing though and only a couple of weeks before I had been in Dingwall, celebrating an escape from the West Coast midges. I had travelled all the way from Aviemore to Stirling purely by bicycle power. Although a bit stiff, I was a lot fitter and had kept going for three consecutive days on the challenging route from Dundee to Kinross without too much trouble.

Fig. 90: 'Beat That' women's samba band

The next destination was Paisley and the home of our daughter Roxanne, partner Stevie and their wee son Conor. Before that though, there was a special visit to make. Nicky from "Beat That", a women's samba band, had phoned whilst I was in Fort William, inviting me to visit them in Stirling and drum with the band. How could I refuse an offer like that? As a lapsed Djembe drummer, the old fingers were itching already and samba drumming was a new adventure. The drill hall where the band met was just round the corner from Mary and John's house. On arrival, the group presented me with some ear plugs and advised me not to put a cup of tea on the windowsill as the vibrations would cause it to jump off. We drummed away for an hour or so and then I headed for Paisley, still with drumming fingers, a big smile and a rhythm in my head.

Jumping on the bathroom scales at Roxie and Stevie's Paisley flat, I'd gained 7lbs/3kg! That habit of eating cakes to keep energy levels up was to blame but dealing with it was just going to have to wait until the journey's end. It was lovely to not only be in a house again, but also with family. There was no need to behave like a visitor, so having grabbed some food I made a dive for the bath, where those stiff muscles relaxed and so did I.

Lee came up to Paisley for a couple of hours and brought the laptop. We spent most of his visit backing up photographs, replying to emails and doing a yarn stocktake. He and Stevie managed to get Blogger to work with the new phone so that I could finally write the blog. Later on, I finished the crocheted rock for the Plockton seals to sit on and they looked great.

There is nothing like spending time with a small person for restoring perspective. We had a great walk around Paisley the following day, including a lengthy stop at a coffee shop. It was strange to be out and about on foot instead of the bike, and those walking muscles were definitely out of practice. This was a real break, as I could hardly ignore our lovely grandson to do paperwork, blogging, crochet and all the other things that usually encroached on a day off.

As an avid reader of travel books, it was interesting to note that all those "famous" cyclists in the books seemed to have a simpler time of it. They were not doing mini workshops, knitting and crocheting what they saw and riding a Brompton like I was. Not many were in their 50s and a bit overweight either. So all in all I was not doing too badly, and what's more, midges and rain were a lot better than extreme heat, hostile conditions or cycling across a desert.

Fig. 91: Roxie and Conor at the Old Mill Waterfalls

day 43, Monday 10th August: Paisley to Lanark and Kirkfieldbank, cycled 14 miles

The trick to city cycling in the UK is to get hold of the relevant Cycle City route map. There is one for each large town in the UK. They make it easy to find quiet routes and reveal a hidden city that motorists and walkers will never see.

apps, sat navs, clouds and other technology

Stirling Bike Hub had told me about a cycling app that could be used as a map. When I downloaded the map however, it was added to the phone as 1,800 individual photographs as well as in the app itself. They were still there after the app had been deleted and all had to be got rid of individually. Never again! Here is my view of apps, clouds and other technology: a paper map still works when you have no phone signal, a flat battery or if it gets wet.

The cycle route from Paisley to Glasgow went along purpose-built cycle ways, through parks, beside rivers and down quiet residential streets. There were nice views with lots of peace and quiet - you would never imagine it was the middle of Glasgow. It was raining heavily in Glasgow and being on familiar ground, I visited a favourite haunt for lunch - Stereo vegan cafe, before hopping on a train to Lanark.

After three nights sleeping in beds, I was camping again. The home-cooked meals at people's houses had been bliss, and eating out had definitely lost its novelty. Lanark had a supermarket though, a luxury as I would often miss them by a few miles whilst cycling. It would have been a good plan to shop on the way to the campsite at Kirkfieldbank, as the hill from the town of Lanark down into the valley was almost vertical, but I was at the bottom before thinking of that. Back up the hill I went to buy groceries therefore, cycling most of it but having to push for a short way due to completely running out of puff.

The supermarket had loads of pre-prepared fruit, veg and other cold food. They were ideal and I went a bit mad, buying fruit salad, melon, salad leaves, cucumber, tomatoes, bananas and apples, whilst of course feeling appropriately guilty about all the packaging again. There had been a number of days when it had simply been a case of keeping going, and at one point I had actually asked Lee to remind me why I was doing this journey. Things were much easier now that there were fewer midges and less rain and I really was hitting my stride. Cafes, cake and trashy knitting novels were still essential for lifting the spirits though. The lack of fresh fruit and veg had obviously taken its toll, so I ate the lot, savouring every mouthful but also going out later for some Chinese food and cycling up that hill yet again.

The next workshop was at New Lanark World Heritage Centre the following day and I would meet up with Lee again in Biggar on Wednesday. So with that thought, listening to the familiar sound of the rain on the tent yet again, I nodded off.

day 44, Tuesday 11ᵗʰ August: New Lanark World Heritage Site, cycled 3.5 miles

workshop number 13

Why would a £250 down sleeping bag not have a full length zip? It was also quite a narrow bag and what with that and the sheet sleeping bag, getting in and out took about five minutes. Having a hot flush in the sleeping bag was not funny, and something in last night's Chinese meal brought them on big time, as well as causing a need for lots of water and consequent trips to the loo.

The campsite would not get any Brownie points for its facilities, which had a run-down feel. There were no sink plugs in any of the washbasins and only one working shower. Overseas travellers often take a universal sink plug with them, but I had never heard of anyone having to do so in the UK.

Most of the site was residential and I chatted with a woman who had lived there for many years. She and her husband loved the friendliness and community spirit of the site, although she said that additional maintenance, more expensive heating bills and having to pay site fees meant it cost more than living in a house.

Fig. 92: the Wallace Cave pub

Lanark was a trip down memory lane - it is the the place where I had held my first 'proper' job as a trainee social worker at the age of 20. When I first moved to the town to start work, the local authority put me up in a children's home for a couple of months. When not at work, I spent time there untangling kite strings, playing games and having a lovely time with the kids. I managed to find the building, which was now flats. The old social work offices where I had actually worked had reverted to their original use as a bank again, but the local pub the Wallace Cave looked just the same and still did tea and biscuits for £1. The landlady Florence used to pull a pint of Guinness and then level the frothy head off with a table knife. 'Strands' yarn shop was also still there. It first opened in the 1960s, which must be something of a record, although it moved from one side of the street to the other in the 1980s.

The New Lanark Heritage site is well known to us Scots, who all learned about Robert Owen's social experiment there at school. He provided decent housing, schooling for the children and working conditions which were better than the norm. He believed that treating workers and their families well would lead to better productivity as well as being more humane. The mill is now a vibrant visitor centre. The original housing is now being lived in again and there is a hotel and youth hostel on site.

Fig. 93: Strands Knitting Shop, Lanark

Yarn is still spun there and as well as the on-site mill shop which sells some yarn along with other things, they now have a website which sells the full range of yarns in a good selection of colours. The shop had some rather nice knitting kits to make cushions that looked like highland cows or rabbits. I had purchased a large quantity of New Lanark yarn for Knit 1 Bike 1 and was aiming to complete the project mainly using British yarn. New Lanark was one of only two yarn producers visited on the trip. The other one was the Border Mill alpaca processors and spinners visited later on in Duns, but I only stumbled across them by chance once I was on the road.

I bumped into Christine by chance in Lanark. I knew her through spinners gatherings and she came along to the workshop as a result of our chance encounter. Two friends from nearer home, Sheila and Maggie, had planned to surprise me by coming along, but Maggie broke her toe and could not drive. A number of visitors came to find out what Christine and I were doing and the workshop took place in a room with The Quaker Tapestry exhibition, which was on display there for a few weeks. So it was a worthwhile and pleasant afternoon, despite being disappointed that there were not more people there.

Fig. 94: New Lanark Heritage Centre

Fig. 95: Christine in the Yarn Shop at New Lanark

day 45, Wednesday 12th August: Kirkfieldbank to Biggar, 16 miles

Up and off by 9.15 this morning, probably the earliest start since cycling from Aviemore to Newtonmore. After dithering a bit over what route to take, I opted for the back road from Kirkfieldbank, marked as a cycle route to Biggar. It would miss out Lanark and avoid the need to cycle up that very steep hill into the town yet again. Minor roads often seemed to go over hills, whilst main roads went round them, so many 'recommended' cycle routes were simply not a good option on a longer journey - hence the dithering. The short but steep roller coaster hills do not really show up on a road map either, so the hills were not always obvious in advance. At least I would be cycling up *different* hills on the cross country route, rather than the same one again though. The first half mile of this route was a whopper of a hill, which seemed almost vertical in places, so no luck there. I had to push the bike for a good bit of it, having ground to a halt because it was so steep. Pushing a fully laden bike up a hill is harder work than cycling up, and it is almost impossible to get back on and get underway again once you get off. The view from the top of the hill made it all worthwhile though and it was easy going from then on.

South Lanarkshire used to be distinctive for its red roads, surfaced using locally quarried stone chips. Most are now covered in the usual black top but I did find a half mile stretch of remaining red surface. As a trainee social worker in the 1980s I had driven these roads in a Strathclyde Region minivan and visited isolated families in the direst of poverty. There would be a handful of council houses in the middle of nowhere, maybe at the side of a reservoir, and a lone parent on benefits living miles from shops, childcare or any hope of a job. They often had to get a taxi in order to buy food. Thankfully, policy changed and people who needed support were eventually offered housing in towns with shops and a social life. I cycled past idyllic-looking bungalows and smallholdings, remembering the isolation, hard winters and heavy snow in those hills.

We ourselves had spent a good many years living in an isolated rural setting and found it to be an expensive and not very environmentally friendly way of life. Living in the village where we are now, eight miles distant from the previous house, means there are amenities and shops within walking distance. There are regular buses to a larger town, so we can go about our lives without having to drive absolutely everywhere. There is a reason why people live in communities, I mused.

It was during a break that I noticed that the soles of my hiking boots were completely worn through. After years of being used for dog walking and occasional longer outings, forty five days of continuous Knit 1 Bike 1 use had proved too much for them. I ordered an identical pair online to make sure they would fit, and arranged for them to be delivered to the campsite at Biggar by next day courier. If only I had noticed before leaving Glasgow, it would have been so easy to buy some. It made me think about outdoor gear in general, because quite a bit of it had worn out on the way. When buying outdoor equipment and clothing, maybe we are really buying the *idea* of doing outdoor activities. The gear itself is not perhaps made to withstand constant use because manufacturers know it will spend most of its life in a cupboard.

Things that were no good or wore out:

- The phone – cracked screen.
- The tent – leaked and had to be proofed. It needed extra guy ropes as well.
- The titanium tent pegs that came with the tent - useless and would not stay in the ground.
- Sleeping bag number 1 – not warm enough.
- Sleeping bag number 2 – leaked down everywhere.
- Sleeping bag number 3 – still in use and warm, but has a zip only half the length of the sleeping bag, despite costing £250.
- Rear pannier – fell to bits.
- Folding hairbrush – fell to bits.
- Expensive cycle glasses – fell to bits. The cheap replacement pair were great
- Cycle shirt – covered in oil. It had served its purpose and was ten years old though
- Watch strap – fell to bits after a month.
- Map case – the Velcro fastening came off so it was no longer waterproof.
- The CTC route planner – used too much phone battery and it was hard to tell where you were.

- The Bike Hub route planning app. Arrgh!
- The bike lock – would not lock.
- And of course the hiking boots.

Biggar and getting the trots...

Now that I was closer to home, it was easier for Lee to come and meet up with me, and frankly we were missing each other. Having spent time together at Dunkeld and seen him briefly in Paisley, I did wonder if it was cheating to meet up again at Biggar. This was always meant to be a pleasurable meander though, rather than a gird-your-loins challenge, so what the heck? I wanted it to be a journey that would inspire others to head off for a weekend's cycling without feeling the need to do fifty miles a day and suffer. And I was still doing the cycling after all, and not being followed around everywhere by a car, which has always seemed a ridiculous idea.

I arrived at Biggar before Lee, so settled into the Church cafe for an hour, hoping to see him driving past with the caravan although I never did. We had a scheduled three night caravan stopover at the campsite there, which is one of our favourites. The stop coincided with the annual Edinburgh Guild of Weavers, Spinners and Dyers Gathering at nearby Broughton, where I would be meeting up with friends and fellow spinners. Time to do the laundry again and dry everything out. Things got damp in the tent no matter what, but the dampness was only noticeable once I was somewhere dry and warm.

Fig. 96: Lanarkshire's red roads are now mostly gone

For several hours I did nothing other than trot to the loos and back again, due to a bit of a tummy upset. The five minute walk (or at times sprint!) from the caravan to the campsite toilets was a trial. Someone up there was looking out for me though, as the tummy upset did not start until I was at the campsite rather than on the road. It was the only health challenge of the whole trip and a minor one at that.

Fig. 97: drying things out at Biggar

day 46, Thursday 13th August: cycled half a mile

It was great how many campsites were near towns, and without them the trip would have been a lot more challenging. The Biggar one was run by the local council and situated in the middle of a park, with a duck pond, golf course and football pitch around the caravans and tents. Many caravans stayed for the whole season, putting up huge awnings. We had fun peeking in to see what they had brought with them. Some had fridges, microwaves and other home comforts. We even spotted a leather three-piece suite in one awning.

There was a club house for the golf course and a wee cafe, both of which did cheap food and did not mind you lingering. Oh bliss. We cycled back to the brilliant Gillespie Church Cafe in Biggar where you could also linger and got cups of coffee and cake for two for only £3.50, buying books for 50p each in their second-hand book store.

Realising that there were only two more camping nights on the itinerary, I re-planned part of the route to go through Duns and Kelso, and booked B&B instead. Lee would take the camping gear home with him and lighten the load a bit. For the rest of the trip I would either be staying with friends, in guest houses or with Lee in the caravan. Yippeee...And of course the weather was far better from then on.

On the crochet front, the Glenfinnan Viaduct was proving a rather large project but was going well, with another three out of the twenty one arches completed during the stay at Biggar. I had not yet worked out how to make it stand up, or attach it to the mountains at either side but would just keep crocheting more archways for now.

day 47, Friday 14th August: Cycled half a mile

We pottered about and went to the Co-op supermarket. The half mile cycle into Biggar felt like very hard work. I had two hot showers just because I could, and got cracking with the usual admin backlog. I re-stocked yarn supplies and planned future crochet projects. Then cleaned and oiled the bike, pumped up the tyres and made phone calls. Laura, who lived in Biggar, dropped by for a visit with her collie dog and we had a good old knitting chat over a cup of tea. We had not met before and she had got in touch when she found out I was in the area. Knitters are so friendly.

We had a simple but yummy sausage, beans and chips at the clubhouse for dinner then spent the evening there chatting, crocheting and just hanging out with other campers – and thankfully my stomach behaved itself.

day 48, Saturday 15th August: the Spinners' Gathering at Broughton, cycled 12 miles.

This wonderful annual Gathering organised by the Edinburgh Guild of Weavers, Spinners and Dyers, involves several Spinning and Weaving Guilds getting together in Broughton village hall to spin and have a good natter. Picture fifty spinning wheels and a lot of cake in a hall, in a tiny village in the middle of nowhere, and you get the picture.

There were specialist suppliers selling fleeces, books and other things for textile enthusiasts. As with many hobbies, there is a whole world out there which those who are not textile enthusiasts would know nothing about. So at gatherings like this one, people were able to stock up on supplies just for spinning, weaving and dyeing, often from a small business run by someone who shared their passion.

I regularly teach spinning courses for one of those suppliers, Scottish Fibres, and they were a supporter of the Knit 1 Bike 1 project. A good number of individual spinners at the Gathering had supported it as well, and it was good to be able to give people a progress report.

I attend the Gathering most years, but this year Knit 1 Bike 1 had its own wee table and I laid out all the half finished crochet and knitting along with the maps and itinerary. The crocheted seals had suffered rather from being carried around, and the whole display looked a bit scruffy. It was impossible to finish and stiffen the work in transit and then stuff it into a bicycle bag again, so it would just have to do. There was lots of interest and several people wanted to know more about Bromptons, folding bikes in general and cycle routes around Scotland. Quite a few people ordered the Knit 1 Bike 1 book in advance which was even better.

Fig. 98: the Spinners' Gathering at Broughton

Being with good friends was wonderful and there were several members there from my own Guild in Dumfries and Galloway. I could not resist buying some fibre of course, and played with my new purchase of multi-coloured green and blue combed merino (called tops), carding it with some fibre from British Black Welsh Mountain sheep. It would be spun to use as yarn for knitted mountains.

Then, having waved goodbye to Sarah, Fiona and other friends, it was back to the caravan site to finish preparations for the following day. I finally let go of the waterproof plastic food box bought on

Arran, which had still only been used to carry oatcakes. It really did take up a lot of room in the bike bag.

Fig. 99: Scottish Fibres at Broughton

There were exactly three weeks to go. I was fit and confident about making it all the way home unless something unexpected happened. The train journey from Glasgow to Lanark was the last time I would use public transport and from now on the whole trip would be done by bicycle. Most nights I would be staying with friends and would have lots of encouragement and company for the rest of the way. But yet again it was hard to get going after a couple of days off. This time I expected it though and just got on the bike and went. With a lighter load by a whole 2kg now that the camping gear had gone home with Lee. Except that I had gained at least that much round the waistline since leaving home, of course.

day 49, Sunday 16th August: Biggar to Edinburgh, 27 miles

Today's ride was an easy one in cycling terms, despite the distance, and was straight down the A702 with few hills. The traffic was busy even on a Sunday and I used the pavement as much as possible to start with. But after dodging several trees, gravel and some very narrow sections, I suddenly came across a missing access chamber cover and a gaping hole, screeching to a halt on the gravel surface just in time. So the only near miss of the whole trip was on the pavement.

I stuck to the road after that and cycled fast, whizzing along at an average 7.5 miles per hour including stops, meaning I probably did ten to twelve miles an hour whilst actually cycling. The rear luggage slowed me down a lot, because it just would not behave without the camping gear in the bag. I must have stopped to adjust it ten times, as it kept swinging round to the side and getting in the way. At one point the rope which secured it came off and luckily I spotted it before it could wrap itself around the chain.

I was staying with my stepmum and good friend Audrey, and she had another friend staying for a few days as well. Yet another friend was joining us for dinner. Then two more friends happened to be passing, so we ended up with an impromptu party, which was just what the doctor ordered. It was nice to be somewhere familiar, feel comfortable enough to help myself in the kitchen and once again spend far too long in the bath. I sometimes wondered if the whole point of cycling was that the bath and food felt so good after all that exercise. The scales were thankfully saying I had not gained any more weight – phew - but I was still several pounds heavier than on leaving home.

day 50, Monday 17th August: the Edinburgh Festival, 12 miles

I did not really want to be bothered with visiting the Edinburgh International Festival, but decided it was necessary from a Knit 1 Bike 1 perspective. Having got as far as Polwarth Terrace just at the start of the city centre, I stopped at a quiet cafe before braving the crowds.

The Royal Mile was ridiculously busy and even pushing the bike along was impossible. Two Star Wars characters were having a heated discussion about a £10 note and Japanese tourists were queuing patiently to have their photos taken with the resident kilt-wearing piper. Outside one of the cafes was a bicycle properly parked in a cycle rack, with a brown envelope tucked into its wheel, saying 'to the owner of this bike' – most intriguing.

That was enough and happily, the Quaker Meeting House was having open house as festival Venue number 40 nearby. The poster in the meeting house was about the Quaker testimony to 'live adventurously' – very apt.

Fig. 100: Star Wars characters

The Meeting House had a pop-up cafe, offering a haven of relative peace and congenial company, as well as being a theatre venue. Everyone was most encouraging and it was nice to meet Quakers from other areas. They even offered me a free ticket to a show –'Raft' but although it was just about to start, there was not quite enough time for me to go to it, as I had a workshop to do that evening.

Fig. 101: the Royal Mile

Fig. 102: Edinburgh Quaker Meeting House venue

workshop number 14: Little Jazz Bird

It was a brisk cycle back to Colinton with a stop at Pins and Needles knitting shop on the way. The shop is another well-established knitting and fabric shop, a bit like Strands in Lanark and it stocks a good range of yarns at different prices. They make up their own knitting kits and had a lovely one for a pair of toddler trousers with a shark's face and teeth on the bum.

Victoria Bennett's house in Dalry was the venue for the evening's workshop. She is a jazz singer part time, so creative in more ways than one (www.littlejazzbird.co.uk, if you want to hear her sing). We had originally met because she came to me for a spindle spinning lesson. Her uncle and aunt turned out to have an amazing bed and breakfast about five miles from where we live, called "The Old School Dalleagles", and that is where my yarn and fibre retreats now take place.

The sun must have affected my brain, because I forgot the knitters attending the workshop wanted a slide show and did not take my computer usb drive. Everyone was very kind about it and we spent a lovely couple of hours talking and knitting. Victoria had everything well organised, despite being in the middle of having her kitchen re-fitted. Actually she no longer had a kitchen, just a bare room. We helped her eat the ice creams from the freezer because the power would be turned off the following day, and discussed various knitting problems that people had brought along.

Fig. 103: Pins & Needles knitting shop

Victoria had recently been to Iceland on holiday, where you could buy 100% wool Lopi yarn in the supermarkets very cheaply. They even sold napkins with a picture of a knitted Icelandic yoke on them which she passed around, although it seemed a shame to use them and I tucked mine into the bicycle bag. Then suddenly it was 9pm and the light was fading. The rear light would not work and must have switched itself on in the bag, running the battery down. I donned the reflective jacket and cycled through Edinburgh as fast as possible, convinced the police would pull me over, making it back to Colinton just before it got really dark.

Fig. 104: the workshop at Victoria's

day 51, Tuesday 18th August. Colinton to Penicuik, 13 miles.

workshop number 15: Penicuik Arts Centre

A rude awakening at Audrey's due to loud shouting outside. It was a group of soldiers from the nearby barracks out jogging, and later on there were bagpipes as they practised for the evening's performance of the Festival's Military Tattoo. When I cycled past an hour or so later, there they were all in full regalia – kilts, busbys and spats, and were piping away in the yard.

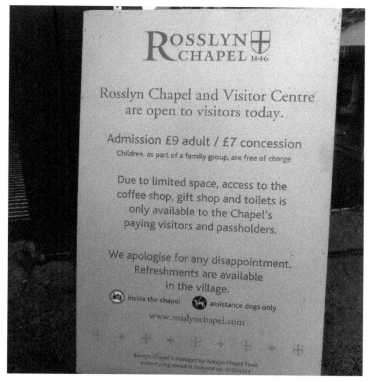

Fig. 105: a notice at Rosslyn

The ten miles to Penicuik took me close to Rosslyn Chapel, made famous by author Dan Brown in his book 'The Da Vinci Code', and I made a three mile detour to visit it. It still operated as an Episcopal church but had a modern visitor centre attached. The first thing that greeted visitors at the door though was a notice stating that you could not use the toilets or cafe unless you paid the £9 admission charge - what a welcome. The restriction was understandable as they do get coach loads of visitors and for some reason the centre was built with very few toilets. But I am afraid I nipped into the loo and explored no further, overwhelmed by a coach load of tourists.

Fig. 106: Di and Ken at Penicuik

The evening's event was a talk and slide show at Penicuik Arts Centre. The Centre was made from two terraced houses knocked together and is a wonderful and friendly place with its own cafe. The upstairs studio had proper wooden floors and an open fireplace and in normal life I regularly teach 'learn to spin' workshops there in association with the Centre and Scottish Fibres.

Fig. 107: the talk at Penicuik Arts Centre

The talk was attended by 16 people, some of whom were knitters, some cyclists and some just interested. I did a reasonable job of it and enjoyed the extensive range of gluten free cakes organised by Di and others on the committee. I was staying with Di and her husband overnight and they made me very welcome. We had met when she attended one of the spinning workshops at the Arts Centre a few months previously. The evening meal of lamb and sweet potato shepherd's pie was accompanied by veg from their own allotment – yummy.

day 52, Wednesday 19th August: Penicuik to Longniddry, 22 miles

Waking early, with a head full of all the things to do on arriving home, I decided to do some planning. Having time to write and work on the artworks for this project had re-charged the old creative batteries somewhat. I had produced a good bit of knitted and crocheted art whilst on the road, even though none of it was actually finished off yet. I would also get home with a complete first draft of the book as I had been writing it up religiously almost every day.

To keep up the feel-good factor once I was home again, I mused, I could spend an hour a day gardening because it had to be done anyway, and an hour cycling to stay fit. Quite a good plan so far. Then an hour doing creative work and writing, and an hour (more like two actually) on the inevitable admin, website and blog, accounts, emails and so on necessary to run a business...but those were just the extras – where did the core business activities of delivering workshops and making things to sell to actually earn a living fit in? Yet again, thinking was not the solution, and it had all fitted in fine before and was perfectly good fun. The stuff about not thinking too much had become a bit of a theme. It was a change for the better as a result of doing the journey. So my advice is dump the 'think it through, figure it out' self help books and go and have some fun. The answers will either come once you are relaxed and enjoying life, or you will just stop bothering about it. Do not give those books to a charity shop for some other poor soul to buy - but they make good fuel if you have a wood burning stove. I would be the first to say that there are *some* good self help books out there – just not *those* ones.

The first proper, paid-for Create With Fibre workshop would take place a few days after getting home. It was to be an open air indigo 'have a go' workshop for the harvest festival at a local country park. Indigo is wonderful stuff. The fabric is still white when it comes out of the dye vat and gradually turns blue on contact with the air. Magical for the kids to see. Then there would be a week's family holiday, followed by a series of eight workshops for Young Scot Ayrshire, where we would be making miniature tipis to go with the festival theme of their annual sponsor's event. In between these, would be several learn to spin day courses and a four day residential spindle spinning course. Not exactly a lot of time to chill in other words, but a full-on fibre and textile business as usual. And I was looking forward to diving in.

Having told Di that I had not got really lost on the whole trip, today was the day when I did. The cycle way from Penicuik to Longniddry was closed at what could have been Bonnyrigg. It was hard to tell, because as usual when you emerge from a cycle track into a town, there was nothing to say which town. A bridge was shut due to building work and the photocopied detour signs put up by Miller Homes were all identical. There was no information about whether to go left or right at any given point and eventually they petered out altogether. I free-wheeled down a very steep hill and came across a sign that said 'entry to house only', so pushed the bike back up the gravel track, which was too slippery to cycle on. A guy at a farm-cum-industrial unit at the top assured me that the track was the way to go, so down I went again with some apprehension, because he added that the man who owned the big house at the bottom was 'kind of funny'.

There were no more cycle route signs, but further on there was a cattle grid, with a rather more definite notice saying 'house only'. It looked like someone's front drive and it was. After going up yet another steep hill, I ended up in the front garden of a rather large house with an old fashioned bell pull. Who could resist? I had always wanted to pull one of those. A perfectly nice man and woman with a Dachshund came to the door, and after we had had a chat, they pointed me back down the hill (sigh!) to a rough, narrow path leading onto the viaduct. This was where I needed to get to and it had been tantalisingly close yet inaccessible at the same time, especially when I had cycled underneath it but just could not get up there.

Having hauled the bike over slippery tree roots and through a patch of mud, there was finally a notice telling me I was heading for the cycle route. It had not been visible from the main track and no wonder I had missed it. Someone at Miller Homes had a twisted sense of humour. From then on it was easy and I was sailing over the viaduct and on towards Dalkeith - where I got lost for the second time.

Fig. 108: the Preston Grange curator

A couple of cyclists going the other way reported that the official, yellow diversion signs in place for that section of the route were hopeless. There was also an additional blocked section on the diversion itself, due to some TV filming taking place in the park. So the road was the better option if only I could get orientated. There was a string of villages together and it was not possible to tell which one I was in, let alone what road it was. After cycling up and down several roads then back to a roundabout, I spotted enough signs to pinpoint where I was on the map and finally set off in earnest.

The road led to Preston Grange outdoor industrial museum. In contrast to Rosslyn chapel, there was a friendly welcome and a great cafe, popular with local dog walkers. The site itself is open air, with mining trucks, boilers, kilns and an amazing beam engine. After tea and sustenance, I got shown around the inside of the beam engine by the seasonal curator on duty, who also worked as a freelance theatre artist. I took some great photos including one of her beside a giant spanner in the beam engine housing.

Fig. 109: old crane at Preston Grange

Near Preston Pans, the old Cockenzie coal-fired power station was being demolished. The power company had promised to tell the locals when the big chimney was coming down so that they could go and watch. There was a raffle to see who got to press the button and I watched a video of it later once I was home. To see the chimneys being demolished go to this link - http://goo.gl/oavHjd – and do check out the official guy wearing the crocheted black and yellow tie!

Fig. 110: an old boiler at Preston Grange

I stopped at the beach there and put a finger in the water, just to be able to say I had truly cycled from one side of Scotland to the other – what a thrill.

Preston Pans is a "mural town" and there were paintings here and there on buildings. The John Muir Way, a coast to coast walking path runs alongside the road in places. The route goes from Helensburgh in the West to Dunbar in the East and covers 134 miles / 215km in total.

Fig. 111: Prestonpans - I had now gone from coast to coast the long way round

I was staying near Longniddry with Angela, Bill and their dog Kai for a couple of nights whilst delivering a long draw spinning workshop to Haddington Spinners. Just before getting to their house, I came across a field with a strange encampment in it. A yurt, some tents, a Citroen Romahome and even a loo tent, all with two ponies looking on curiously. A road protest? A peace camp? No – it was Haddington Spinners, who were camping out in Angela's horse field. Isabella was justly proud of her frame tent, bought on EBay for £1 and I was impressed – it was hard to imagine my local group, Ayrshire Handspinners camping out in a field.

Fig. 112: Angela, Bill and Kai and Longniddry

But I had a luscious bed for the night and Angela and I joined the group after I'd had a hot bath, in a bathtub so large my feet did not touch the end. I even managed to get a tiny bit of crochet done, but now having some completed things to show people, I was getting a bit complacent. This resulted in a slower work rate and that needed to change. I resolved to post all the finished work home and focus on crocheting the Glenfinnan Viaduct.

day 53, Thursday 20th August, workshop

workshop number 16: long draw with Haddington Spinners

Actually, we did more extended draw spinning than long draw, which for those of us who are spinners is an important difference. If you are American that's English long draw to you. You non-spinners can ignore this bit because you will not care anyway.

The Spinners had brought along their Great, or Muckle Wheel, plus a smaller home-made version made from a bicycle wheel and wood found in Isabella's shed. It is called a 'Thrifty Fox', and plans for how to make one can be found on www.ravelry.com - a social networking site for those who knit and crochet. The weather was perfect and we were out in the field all day. Group member Debbie Zawinski had written a book about Scottish native sheep breeds, 'In The Footsteps of Sheep', which was to be published shortly after I returned home. She had knitted a giant sock with wool from native breeds which she brought along by special request to show me.

Fig. 113: Debbie with her giant sock

Fig. 114: Haddington spinners - a lively bunch

Angela and I went to the beach later on and spent a happy hour scrabbling about amongst great piles of shells looking for that special one. My best find was a piece of gnarled green glass just like the one I had been shown at the Newton Grange Museum. They are common on the beaches in the area and a waste product from old glass factories. Angela found a piece of polished coal, almost like jet, left over from the coal-fired power station just by the beach.

A scrummy seafood dinner followed and an evening of chatting and crocheting the Glenfinnan Viaduct. I had the makings of another two arches done by bedtime. Angela looked the viaduct up on the Internet and reported that it definitely had twenty one arches and they were built out of concrete. There had been a story that someone had died during the construction and was still inside one of the arches. In the 1990s someone used a special camera and checked, finding nothing. Another one nearby, the Loch Nan Uamh Viaduct apparently turned out to have a horse and cart in its large central pillar though. Wow – no hope that I could get away with just doing half a dozen of the arches as a token gesture now then. I had completed four, which was a start. Only seventeen to go and the biggest job had been working out how to make them.

day 54, Friday 21st August: Longniddry to Innerwick, 24 miles

The highlight of today's cycle was finding two giant puffballs at the side of the cycle track. I had always wanted to see some and no one other than a cyclist would have spotted these ones. People on Facebook asked if I had picked them. I could not bring myself to do it and learned afterwards that you can slice a bit off to cook and leave the rest to spore in peace.

The day's journey followed Sustrans Route 76. Having worked out a route on the map, I knew it was possible to get *almost* all the way to Innerwick without having to cycle on the A1. There was a tiny gap on the map though, with no road or track shown, going past the cement works at Dunbar. I was hoping the cycleway had been extended to connect the missing section but would not know until I got there. If the route did not work it would mean a long detour back the way I had come.

Fig. 115: giant puffballs on the way to Innerwick

The gamble paid off and I avoided cycling over steep hills inland on the only other possible route. Cycle Route 76 had indeed been extended to go behind the cement works, then emerged onto a track following the A1, close to Torness power station. I was not quite sure which junction to take to Innerwick and phoned Jenni's house. Her son Finn answered the phone and gave excellent directions, saving me a lot of bother.

I arrived at Jenni and Richard's house with a terrible craving for sweet things and very hungry. It was lovely to see Jenni again and to meet her hubby Richard and their delightful children Finn and Morven. It was a very relaxing stay indeed, with the usual access to hot baths, lots of food and good company. Jenni and Richard are both archaeologists and live in a very old house which is upside down, with the living area at the top and bedrooms underneath. The rest of the household consisted of Lottie, the world's most laid back greyhound, and two cats.

Fig. 116: Jenni, Richard, Finn and Morven with Lottie the lurcher

day 55, Saturday 22nd August: two weeks to go

workshop number 17: Innerwick

The workshop today, organised by Jenni, was on 'yarn pooling'. This is what sometimes happens when you knit with multi-coloured and hand dyed yarns. One or more of the colours decide to congregate in one place creating a 'pool' of colour. It is not necessarily a problem and can look quite nice, but it was fun to play and get different effects. We all met in Innerwick Village Hall and had a lovely afternoon learning how to influence the appearance of colours by using different stitches (eg moss stitch), changing the number of stitches and a few other tricks with multicoloured yarns. Some of the effects people got were great and there was lots of enthusiasm along with the inevitable cups of tea and chat.

Then we headed back to Jenni's for a relaxing time, during which I crocheted a door for a derelict mouse hole in their outside back porch, just for fun. The viaduct was also doing well and maybe I was learning how to focus on one project at a time. Then again, maybe not...

At bedtime I pondered, very briefly, the fact that being really tired makes it so much easier to just switch your brain off and go to sleep.

Fig. 117: the workshop at Innerwick

day 56, Sunday 23rd August: Innerwick to St Abbs, 16 miles

After a straightforward hour and a half's cycling from Innerwick, I came across a caravan site which turned out to have a cafe and public beach access. It was a beautiful surfing beach with views across the bay and I lingered for a while with a cup of tea and brunch.

Fig. 118: the results of the 'yarn pooling' workshop

Immediately afterwards, the road and Sustrans Route 76 took an extremely steep uphill turn. There was no alternative route other than the busy A1. A bloke at the caravan site said he had struggled to get up it in his Ford Transit so what chance did I have? I managed to cycle up most of the steepest part and only pushed the bike for a couple of hundred yards near the top. I hope Van Man was watching.

Still following Route 76, the views were lovely but really what were Sustrans thinking? There were steep hills for miles. So for the next hour it was a stiff uphill slog in a very strong headwind. Little did I know that the wind would bug me for the next three days of cycling as well. On the very steep sections I had to get off and push several times, partly because of the wind.

At the top of Coldingham moor it was flat but the gusts were so strong I still had to get off and push so as not to get blown over and the wind brought me to a complete stop several times. It was a bit surreal at the top. First, there were loud bangs because a guy in a field was shooting at fake birds on sticks. He was a bit close for comfort and with such strong winds I did wonder if his bullets would go where he meant them to. There was nothing to do but push quickly on. Then I cycled through a wind farm, the huge turbines towering over me on both sides of the road, turning in a leisurely fashion, with a barely audible shooshing sound, despite the strong wind.

Fig. 119: St. Abbs - Louise in her conservatory

A farm I was cycling past had a sign pronouncing that it was the 'home of Moondance Wools' which had to be worth a visit. I pushed the bike downhill on a loose gravel track to get there, because it was too tricky a surface for cycling. After negotiating a rather difficult cattle grid with a metre high drop to a stream underneath and talking nicely to two dogs, I got there to find Moondance was closed. So back I went, pushing the bike back up the slippery track and managing the cattle grid rather better this time. It *would* have been an exhilarating free wheel from the top of the moor for several miles – except that the head wind was so strong I still had to pedal even going downhill. Nonetheless it was an easy cycle to Coldingham as, after the road levelled out, the wind thankfully dropped. I rewarded myself with a visit to the tea shop in St Abbs – too much reward really, though I managed yet again to resist the bronze cast dormice in the gallery next to the cafe, spotted on a previous visit.

For the next two nights, I was staying with Louise at Woolfish and would be spending time with her knitting retreat visitors, who would arrive the following day. She had a B&B guest that first night and the three of us had a nice time chatting over some wine. The wine affected the Glenfinnan Viaduct project a bit though, as some of the arches seemed to come out a different height to the ones I had finished earlier.

Louise had given me an enormous bed with a skylight window above it, so I lay and watched the stars for a while before falling asleep. It was exciting to have made it to St Abbs, which I had previously considered too far away from home to cycle to.

day 57, Monday 24th August: a day off

Another comfy bed meant that I was really catching up on some sleep, but I still woke up tired. The combination of being in a different bed almost every night for several weeks and the previous day's physical exertion, had taken its toll. I spent a luxurious morning reading and napping in bed and finally emerged at lunchtime. The two women had arrived for their knitting retreat and frankly I wished I could join them and just get a lift to Hawick on Thursday. It was very tempting and I was a bit fed up with constantly moving on.

The crocheted viaduct seemed endless – and was to continue to be so for a good few weeks even after returning home. As feared the night before, all of the arches were definitely not the same height and measuring them by eye had not been my best idea. How the dickens would I crochet the hills and base to make sure it all stood upright? Maybe I should start again. It would need to be made in three sections, as the finished and stiffened thing would otherwise be too big to transport or to store in my miniscule studio. So I would also have to work out how to join them together. I'd much rather have forgotten that viaduct and been knitting socks right then.

Instead, it was time to write a proper pattern for the arches, to ensure that future ones were all the same height.

day 58, Tuesday 25th August: St Abbs to Duns, 15 miles

Fig. 120: saying goodbye to Louise

For once I just cracked on despite a strong headwind, with only one wee stop for a bag of crisps and a banana. I actually managed to avoid cakes, trying to break the habit which was hard to resist when I needed to stop in cafes in order to eat, was ravenous and in need of an instant energy boost.

Tonight's stay was at the Swan Hotel at Duns. It was friendly and a very good price, if a touch basic and I got there at 12.30 after only two hours of cycling. The Inn was old and the floor of the room slanted at a jaunty angle – a very strange feeling when sitting on the loo! The hotel staff could not have been nicer and let me into the room straight away even though it was still early. The bike was treated like a special guest and safely corralled in a deserted dining room, where I was assured they would keep an eye on it.

Having enjoyed staying with friends for the last few nights it was now lovely to have an anonymous room and just do my own thing. It was all about balance as usual – enough solitude, enough company, enough roughing it and enough comfort. And more than enough to eat. By the time I had wallowed in the usual deep bath and had a picnic in the room for lunch, it was three o'clock. I jumped on the bike again to visit the Border Mill down the road, a treasure that Haddington Spinners had just happened to mention.

Fig. 121: alpaca drying at the Border Mill

The mill processes alpaca, and many producers send their fibre there for washing, carding and spinning. They also produce their own range of yarns and fibres for sale in lovely colours. I was shown all round the Mill, despite the owner being stung by a wasp and the alpaca washing machine flooding whilst I was there. The place is well worth a visit but not yet widely publicised, as they have concentrated on building up the alpaca processing side of the business first. Look out for their hand-dyed fibres and yarns at the Edinburgh Yarn Festival though, and they do welcome visitors.

Fig. 122: the mill's hand-dyed yarns and fibres

The Swan's basic-looking bar provided an absolutely delicious dinner at a very reasonable price. It was also for once a bar where you could linger without pressure, and I passed a happy evening sitting there and crocheting.

day 59, Wednesday 26th August: Duns to Kelso, 17 miles

ten days to go...

Tonight's B&B owner had texted to say that she would not be home from work until 5pm. This was not handy given the weather forecast and the fact that I only had seventeen miles to cycle. It was a shame she had not told me that when I booked. I left the hotel and headed for a coffee shop across the road, to while away an hour before setting off. A lucky conversation with two fellow knitters there meant I was able to plan a less hilly route, which was just as well because the wind was even stronger than the day before. I told them about Border Mills and they were surprised they had not heard of it. When I left they were busy planning a visit.

I plodded on steadily in second and third gear for most of the way, and the wind made it the equivalent of cycling uphill all day. Stopping at Swinton only a few miles from Duns, I sat on a bench for a snack and a woman came out of her house and presented me with a cup of tea! The Duns/Kelso leg of the journey was definitely the friendliest. Car drivers were especially courteous and patient and even smiled and waved as they went by.

I spotted a cafe in Kelso and went in with mince and tatties on my mind. A lovely welcome and an insistence that I stay as long as I liked, when I mentioned the B&B not being open till 5pm. And joy of joys, the 'special' of the day was mince and potatoes. Kelso was full of Honda Goldwing motorcycles, there for their 34th annual rally in the town. There was also a cycle shop which had just one yellow shirt the right size, to replace mine which was covered in oily marks.

The B&B was in a housing estate and I was in what had probably been their daughter's bedroom. The room had wallpaper, a duvet set and lampshades all depicting hunting scenes in pink – very kitsch. However it was blissfully quiet, spotlessly clean and had its own bathroom. Ideal, in other words. I was not sure whether I was supposed to stay in the room or join them. Being so tired it was academic anyway, and I slept well in the very comfortable bed, emerging in the morning to find that my room key was still on the outside of the door. The couple were going to work and I had to have breakfast by 8am and then let myself out of the front door later on. They were very nice when I met them properly first thing the following day, and had been a bit surprised I did not re-emerge to join them for a chat the night before. Definitely a good B&B for cyclists.

day 60, Thursday 27th August: Kelso to Hawick , 20 miles

a rendezvous - will I ever get there?

Still tired after ten hours of sleep, I set off at 9am. The first half of the journey was fine and I took it easy, stopping at a garden centre for tea and the inevitable cake. Only to find that the wind had got up again and was against me for the remaining ten miles.

Lee and I were meeting up in Hawick. All done-in after struggling against the strong wind, I even wondered if I should phone him to come and get me. Instead, I tried stopping for a brief rest every ten minutes and made better progress, though still seldom getting out of third gear. I made it to Hawick at 3.30, really knackered but recovered quickly after a hot shower.

Lee had the caravan all set up and was just deciding whether to come and find me, having picked up the text message I had sent him about the wind. We would be together in the caravan for the next three days again and I would be seeing a lot more of him for this final part of the journey. We had purposely set it up so that I would have more company for the final few days, thinking these would seem the longest ones of the whole trip. How right that was!

In the evening, there was time to finish crocheting the next five viaduct legs, then I put them aside and decided to work on something else. Crocheting the strawberry sponge cake from the evening with the Mallaig group was next on the list, and the brightly coloured cotton yarn provided a bit of light relief after the grey Aran wool of the viaduct.

day 61, Friday 28th August: into Hawick and back, 3 miles

We got up at 8am and got to work, updating the power point presentation for the day's talk at the Textile Tower House in Hawick.

Fig. 123: the Textile Tower House, Hawick

There was just time to pack up and have a quick lunch before setting off for the centre of town. Lee came too on his red Brompton and was impressed that I had managed to cycle so far the previous day against the wind, which was still strong.

Workshop no.18: the Textile Tower House

The Textile Tower House is special in being a museum and exhibition space dedicated to textiles. Shaureen had organised the workshop, but her colleague Richard was there instead of her on the day, as she was carrying out her other duties as a Registrar. The group were chatty and friendly and had a considerable amount of knitting and crochet expertise between them. Some had contributed to exhibits at the Museum, such as a lovely knitted mural above the stairs. I showed the slide show which seemed to go down well. People crocheted and knitted throughout and one group member gave me a crocheted flower to add to my exhibition. The evening was followed by an equally pleasant meal with Shaureen and Richard. Both were keen cyclists, with Shaureen doing triathlons and Richard cycle touring, so there was much swapping of stories.

Fig. 124: a knitted mural in the Borders Textile Tower House

day 62, Saturday 29th August: a week to go... am I really nearly home?

So how *do* you crochet a strawberry sponge cake? With Rico Essentials cotton double knitting yarn in yellow, red and white, and a 3mm hook, of course. I was working it out as I went but so far so good. The plate was crocheted after I got home, using the same yarn in beige and red, then it was stiffened. I loved the plate – it really worked. I was grateful that someone at a workshop en route had told me about Paverpol liquid, which can be used to stiffen knitting and crochet and even make it weatherproof.

Fig. 125: art work in the cafe opposite the Tower House

Fig. 126: clogs at the campsite in Hawick

The campsite had functioning wifi which was almost a first. So despite having resolved to take a day off I was able to deal with all sorts of things, replying to people about workshops, putting things on Facebook and sorting out the blog which had seen a lot less action than it should have. Then we went for a walk along the river – a real treat, as I had hardly walked anywhere since setting off.

Opposite us on the campsite were a Dutch couple who actually wore those carved wooden clogs when they were walking around the site, instead of the Crocs favoured by most campers. The site was full but thankfully peaceful at night and it was good to have some time in one place again, after three days of cycling. And because it was mostly a day off, no more writing for me, that's it folks.

day 63, Sunday 30st August: Hawick to Langholm, 23 miles

A blissful and relatively speedy 23-mile cycle along quiet roads today, with hardly any hills and no wind. Dumfries and Galloway at last, and now it really did feel like I was on the home straight. Lee actually followed me in the caravan for the first time today so that I had the caravan to sleep in at night. The campsite at Langholm was on the rugby pitch and I had pictured being the only tent on a deserted site, with local youths coming along at night in their cars. Hmm. I stopped for a break in a lay-by and Lee came along, so we got out the deck chairs and had a picnic at the side of the road. Then on I went, dodging the traffic to take a photo of the bike beside the 'Welcome to Dumfries and Galloway' road sign. A real milestone! The campsite at Langholm felt slightly surreal, being on the rugby pitch. It seemed like we were the only folk there apart from one local retired chap, although there were some caravans in storage along one edge of the field. It was peaceful though and with only a few midges.

Then Elderly Gentleman Number 1 - the warden who looked after the site - arrived with his dog Honey and stayed for a long chat. Elderly Gentleman Number 2 - the retired chap from the caravan, soon came along and joined in of course. The site warden had planted trees around Loch Doon and Dalmellington in the 1970s, close to where we live. The other chap had more recently worked as a "forwarder", someone who drives an all-terrain vehicle during tree harvesting in order to get the felled trees down to the road. He had felled the same trees the warden had planted!

The site warden told us that he and his tree-planting co-workers used to be taken up to Dalmellington by minibus on Mondays and were brought home again on Fridays, being accommodated in between times by local people. One day they managed, with a stick, to coax an adder into a bottle and took it on the mini bus with them. Someone took the cork out on the bus and the adder escaped, but they managed to shoo it out of the bus and it swam away up a nearby river. This was the 1970s and before adders were protected, poor things, but what a story! So now I probably had an adder to crochet...

Fig. 127: welcome to Dumfries & Galloway

day 64, Monday 31ˢᵗ August: into Langholm and back, 1 mile

workshop number 19: Blue Moon

The workshop at Blue Moon craft shop and cafe in Langholm coincided with their monthly knitting and crochet group, which was ideal. Blue Moon is something of a community resource and meeting place, because Laura who owns it is just that sort of person.

Fig. 128: with the caravan at Langholm

The knitting and crochet group was taught and led by the very capable Granny Margaret, who was crocheting a splendid, brightly coloured blanket in spike stitch. Others were trying out Tunisian crochet and one member had knitted a beautiful lacy cowl with some of my hand dyed yarns. Blue Moon had been selling the yarns, along with copies of my previous book, 'How To Spin Just About Anything'. We had a go at 'i cord' edging, practised joining pieces of knitting using mattress stitch, and ate cake and drank coffee. I cord was probably invented by the legendary knitter Elizabeth Zimmerman and is a way of knitting a tubular edge using only two needles. It looks a bit like French, or bobbin knitting.

Audrey had come along to the group that day for the first time, aiming to learn to crochet, and she got on very well. (Lee and I would meet her again the following day when we had breakfast at a cafe next to the caravan site. She had carried on with her crocheting and was delighted that the stitches had become more even with practice.) Laura's daughter came into the shop after school and showed off some of her craft skills. And Scott, a member of Dumfries Guild of Weavers, Spinners & Dyers turned up to say hello. It was a real boost to see him and it added to the feeling of being nearly home.

I showed off the half-finished viaduct and the crocheted strawberry cream sponge cake, then Lee joined me and we had fish and chips for tea. I was a bit apprehensive about the following day's cycle from Langholm to Kirtlebridge, which was only 15 miles but would go over the moors and might be another strenuous ride. It was also the one stretch where I thought there might be free-range cows, something I am not at all keen on.

Fig. 129: Laura and her daughter at Blue Moon in Langholm

day 65, Tuesday 1st September: Langholm to Kirtlebridge, 15 miles.

what had I got out of this journey so far?

Memories to treasure and amazement about how much there was to see so close to home. A feeling of greater self-sufficiency because I did most of it solo, albeit with the help and support of others. It made me less fearful and more adventurous. At 57, I learned that I could still camp and that cycling longer distances was fine, which was in doubt before planning the project. All the aches and pains had finally disappeared, I was fit and I now had a resting pulse of 60.

I only had to deal with one day at a time, which is of course what we should all be doing anyway. The only things to worry about were the weather, camping, cycling, writing and crochet. I learned that it was just as hard to get out of the door/tent and onto the bike every day whilst away on a trip as it was at home, but once I was out there it was fine, and routines and habits helped a lot.

Having managed with so little, I could see how much time and mental energy the excess belongings at home had taken up. Before, it had seemed sensible to keep things that might come in handy one day. Now I saw excess stuff for the burden it was, and it would have to go. We had kept an eye on our stuff levels, de-cluttered every time there was a lifestyle change and had a policy of 'one in, one out' for years. But I swear extra stuff crept into the house under cover of darkness, as it accumulated regardless. And being away had made me want even less. I only had one change of clothes with me and it was plenty.

a great day

The cycle over the hills to Kirtlebridge was really good. The hills were not too hilly and the sun was out for the first part of the day. I stopped for a snack at the top and admired the view whilst doing some writing, thinking and generally feeling that all was well with the world. Then I stopped again at The Kirtle pub in Eaglesfield, which had re-opened only four months before and had a cafe as well. I was glad to see it, as there had been nowhere else to eat on the way. It was by then raining heavily and my host for the night, Sarah, would not be home for some time. The Kirtle's fish and chips turned out to be some of the best, with hand-cut chips, a piece of fish the size of a whale and a nice big pot of tea.

Whilst I was there, two men turned up in a white van, trying to sell the young woman owner chef's knives, generators and tool kits. The knives were £80 a set and out of curiosity I looked them up online, to find identical sets for sale at £7.99 a box. The £200 trolley toolbox was for sale online at £79.99. So I was sitting across the room pulling faces at the owner and hoping to get the message across before she succumbed to the very strong pressure to buy, which fortunately she did not. The guys were intimidating, hard to get rid of and left with bad grace. I like to think I contributed to the lack of a sale and the owner gave me a discount on my lovely meal as a thank you for the moral support.

After chatting for a while longer, I cycled the last few miles to Sarah's house near Kirtlebridge, where eight friends were due to congregate later for a good old knit 'n' natter. Sarah is a member of Dumfries & Galloway Guild and had offered to put me up for the night and organise the evening's get together.

workshop number 20: Sarah's house

I was looking forward to spending time with friends, and Sarah had arranged for a reporter from "Dumfries and Galloway Life" – who happened to be her sister in law - to visit as well. After a nice tea with Sarah and two mutual friends Fiona and Anne, the others joined us for an evening of knitting and chat. It was good to catch up and have some time together. Sarah presented me with a hot water bottle at bedtime and I snuggled down feeling really cosy and determined to use it no matter how warm I got.

Fig. 130: the Kirtle at Eaglesfield

day 66, Wednesday 2nd September: Kirtlebridge to Barnsoul, near Dumfries, 28 miles

a parrot, Radio West Sound and lots of dogs

Having got so far, the plan on this final leg of the journey was to cycle every day and just get home. So the final five days were non-stop cycling, starting the previous day – day 65. After having breakfast with Sarah at 7.30, she headed off to work and I snuggled back under the duvet for a bit of rest and relaxation and to crochet a cup cake to leave as a wee thank you for her. Then I cycled a whole four miles before stopping to visit Fiona and her six dogs. She had been at the workshop the evening before and I had always wanted to meet the dogs, having heard so much about them. They all had different stories because she volunteers for The Dogs' Trust. Bobby the chihuahua had the best story of all though.

Fig. 131: Fiona with one of her dogs

He had been totally unmanageable and had been at Battersea Dogs Home and then a rescue centre in Wales, neither of which did very well with him. Fiona had spotted him on a TV show several years previously, where a "dog expert" had also failed to get him to behave. She got in touch and he came to stay with her, living with her happily ever after, and is now very well behaved indeed.

I reached Brow Well and ate lunch on a bench beside the well itself. Brow Well was visited by Scotland's National Bard and poet, Robert Burns, in 1796, on the advice of his doctors. He was told to drink the waters as a cure, but died a few weeks later. Whether or not the water contributed to an early death is debatable, but there are notices advising visitors not to drink the water. It started to rain heavily a short while later and I arrived at Dumfries dripping wet. The Radio West Sound offices were in the shopping precinct, and after dithering for several minutes, I plucked up the courage to go in and ask if they wanted to interview me. They did and recorded a two minute slot for the four o'clock news. The interview took place in a radio studio, but the woman who spoke to me recorded it on her iPhone, explaining that it worked just as well as all the complicated equipment, which they seldom used any more.

Fig. 132: the Brow Well visited by the Scots poet Robert Burns

Further down the precinct, a guy from Parrot Rescue was out and about with an Amazon Orange Tip. The parrot was eleven years old and would probably live until he was about eighty five. He was a real sweetie but had come to the Rescue centre because he kept biting people. The answer apparently was to hand feed him porridge, talk to him and keep him busy, because parrots get bored easily and then get depressed, just like people do.

Fig. 133: parrot rescue, Dumfries

Another snack was called for before tackling the final four miles to Barnsoul caravan park. I was pretty exhausted and just wanted to get to the caravan and crash out. There was a great cycle route alongside the busy A75 but it was closed, and the last few miles were an unpleasant uphill slog in heavy traffic. Being so tired meant getting off every few minutes for a rest, and the pedal crank had developed an annoying squeak again.

workshop number 21: Karen and Carl

Lee was at the campsite waiting and after a hot shower I felt a lot better, although for the first time on the whole journey, rather homesick. We got chatting to Karen and Carl in the washing up area. They were in a campervan and Karen had just bought some knitting needles and yarn in a charity shop but could not quite remember how to knit. So they visited us in the evening for an impromptu session, fulfilling an ambition of mine to hold a workshop in our tiny Freedom Microlite caravan.

Fig. 134: impromptu workshop in the caravan with Karen and Karl

day 67, Thursday 3rd September: Barnsoul to Castle Douglas, 11 miles

A pleasant evening with Carl and Karen had led to an 11.30pm bedtime, and that meant a sluggish start to the day. I nearly wimped out, groaning 'I can't do it any longer'. The mere fact that there was someone there to listen – i.e. Lee – may have had something to do with it. After all, if you are on your own, there is not much point in complaining.

After a restful morning crocheting a gypsy cream biscuit, I set off at 12.40. Strangely, although the tiredness remained it did not affect my ability to cycle, and it was an enjoyable ride. The hills were no bother and the bike was running more freely after a thorough clean-up the day before. That annoying squeak, which had kept me company on and off since the gravel cycle way from Longniddry to Innerwick, was still there though.

Fig. 135: cleaning the bike at Barnsoul

So I stopped and started, oiled and cleaned some more as I went and finally tracked the noise down to some grit that had got in where the Brompton folding pedal meets the crank. This rotates as you pedal, and scraping the dirt out with the tip of a penknife helped, although it returned periodically for months to come before finally disappearing. No wonder some cyclists avoid gravel tracks.

A halfway stop at Hardgate was delightful. The village shop had closed down since my last visit and although the pub had just finished serving meals, the nice woman in charge rustled up an amazing vegetable risotto with chips and salad anyway. I told her about Knit 1 Bike 1 and she declared that this was her day for weird customers. Apparently, the person who had just come in before me had been a seventy-year-old woman from the Lockerbie area, who had just returned from a month-long trek across Mongolia. She had simply got on a plane and gone, then bought a horse from a Mongolian farmer when she arrived. She left her suitcase with him and set off. Although she had ridden in the past, she had apparently not done so for some years. What a shame I had missed her.

With the wind behind me, I sailed into Castle Douglas, back on home turf at last, and had a nice chat with Pauline who owns Sunrise Wholefoods there, a favourite haunt of ours. Kerry who works there makes needle felt pictures and had just had her first solo exhibition, a roaring success. Pauline and Kerry had both been following my adventures on Facebook and it was good to catch up.

I bought some posh olives for Margaret, a fellow spinner and long-time friend who was putting me up for the night. When she cooked a delicious vegetable dish, I realised I had been craving vegetables again and gobbled it up hungrily. We spent a happy evening comparing textile projects – mine the inevitable crocheted Glenfinnan Viaduct, strawberry sponge cake and gypsy cream, and Margaret's projects were some beautiful weaving and a knitted waistcoat. She thought the gypsy cream was a beef burger in a roll, which I realised it could well have been!

day 68, Friday 4th September: Castle Douglas to Hawkrigg campsite, New Galloway, 21 miles

friends on the road

Having said goodbye to Margaret at about 10am, I fully intended to get a reasonably early start for the second-to-last day. But why break a habit after so long on the road? A barbecue was planned at Jane and Andrew's campsite that night and it would not do to be too early and get in the way of the preparations. So I popped back to Sunrise and bought some veggie burgers for the party, just managing to squeeze them into the bike bag.

Then someone bellowed "hello Janet", and it was Karen and Carl from Barnsoul campsite, who invited me to join them for breakfast. We adjourned to the Scottish Pantry for one of their legendary fry ups and a right old chinwag, then who should come in but Maggie and Sheila from my regular craft group at Carsphairn. So it ended up being a bit of a do and I finally left Castle Douglas nearer lunchtime, feeling just so grateful for all the wonderful friends who had helped me on the way - and rather full up after all that food. Sheila and Maggie had continued to be key supporters throughout the journey. They attended the workshop on Day One at the Burns Heritage Museum and had 'liked' just about everything I put on Facebook. They told others about the trip and had tried to come to the New Lanark workshop, until Maggie broke her toe. Sheila had sent me lots of messages en route and the two of them had helped to organise this evening's barbecue party along with Jane and Andrew.

The ride was unexpectedly strenuous, or maybe it was having two breakfasts that did it. I had estimated that it was fourteen miles, but Jane and Andrew were nearer to Carsphairn than New Galloway, making it more like 21. Having delayed setting off, I now became worried that people would arrive early and I would not be there to greet them.

Stopping in New Galloway for a break, I bumped into yet another friend, Archie from our home village of Dalmellington. He and Louise were staying in a holiday cottage nearby for a few days and he was very surprised to see me, having heard about the journey. So I just decided to relax, enjoy the day and not rush. There were rather more hills than expected anyway and it was silly to spoil the penultimate day's cycling by worrying. I stopped again at the Galloway Sailing Centre for a look, having driven past it for years and never got around to visiting. They had a great tearoom overlooking the loch, with enormous slabs of cake at a very good price, which I actually managed to resist, thinking of the evening's buffet.

Fig. 136: arriving at Hawkrigg caravan site

After telling Karen and Carl that there were a couple of campsites on the road to Carsphairn I was surprised to note that there were actually lots. There were the Ken Bridge Hotel and Loch Ken main campsites, plus three Certificated Sites, including Jane and Andrew's one where I would be spending the night. Jane and Andrew were building their house entirely by themselves and had started a poultry smallholding, selling free range eggs.

At 4pm I finally made it to Hawkrigg. Lee was there with the caravan and had thankfully brought a gazebo along for the party, as the wind had got up and a steady drizzle set in. Andrew and Jane had been busy making food with their friends and Maggie and Sheila had put up bunting then gone back home to get yet more food. I made cups of tea in the caravan for everyone which at least made me feel useful. Then we set about fixing extra guy ropes to the gazebo to stop it taking off in the wind, and after that it was steady as a rock, despite the strong gusts.

It was a great evening and Jane had decorated cupcakes, which said Knit 1 Bike 1 on them in icing. So after resisting the cake at the Sailing Centre I pigged out on wine, sausages, veggie burgers and far too much cake - but it would have been rude not to after all. The wind kept the midges at bay and we stayed outside until it got too cold, then sat round the wood burning stove in Jane and Andrew's big kitchen.

Fig. 137: Knit 1 Bike 1 cup cakes

Fig. 138: a welcome home party at Hawkrigg

day 69, Saturday 5th September: home at last, 14 miles

It was weird to think that I would sleep in my own bed tonight. I no longer felt like I *had* a home or bed of my own, and despite never having been away from home for more than a couple of weeks before, I had not really missed the actual house, just the people.

Setting off at about 11am, I resolved to savour every moment of that last day. After cycling half a mile, a car passed me tooting madly, then parked on the verge ahead. Out jumped a friend, Gina! We hugged, chatted and generally caught up a bit. The last time I had seen her, she had just found out that she was pregnant, and now her daughter was a year old.

I stopped at the shop-cum-cafe in Carsphairn to buy cakes, before going on to meet the goats at Maggie's place. The goats are mostly cared for by her two teenagers Bekah and Reuben, who are keen smallholders. The family share goat and chicken care with a good neighbour, and were all busy mucking out when I arrived.

Fig. 139: Bekah and Reuben with the goats at Carsphairn

I forgot to give them the cakes and dropped them off at Sheila's house a few doors down, carefully avoiding her dog, which apparently dislikes anyone wearing yellow. Then I cycled most of the ten miles from Carsphairn to Dalmellington saying 'I did it' to myself over and over and getting a bit tearful every so often. I stopped a few times just to savour the view and make the final few miles last a little bit longer.

It was strange cycling into the village, where there was hardly anyone about. For the first time ever I made it all the way up the steep hill to our street without getting off the bike. Marna from the Knit and Natter group went by in a taxi and spotted me, so the word would be out that I was home.

Lee was just coming out of the door with *his* Brompton when I got to the house, planning to come and take a photo of me arriving in the village. I bravely volunteered to cycle back down the hill for a photo call. We passed Stephen from our street with a bunch of his mates on the way, and Lee shouted "She's just cycled round Scotland", to which the answer was 'aye right' and Lee added "She has, ask your mum about it!"

We took a photo in front of the Dalmellington sign and I cycled up the hill for a second time, no bother. This time Marion from down the road also spotted me and I got a wee cheer before going indoors and finally climbing into the last hot bath of the journey.

Fig. 140: Dalmellington at last

The next day I leapt out of bed thinking 'where am I going today?' before realising I was home, and it took several nights to settle down properly. Every time I looked at the weeds in the garden and the pile of paperwork on the desk I wanted to get on the bike and go away again.

There was only a week at home before we headed off to Aviemore for a family holiday. Whilst there, we re-visited the Active Cafaidh to tell them I had made it all the way home and of course to get some free porridge and a cooked breakfast.

In Aviemore, I bought an ultra lightweight camping mattress along with a wee gadget that turned it into a chair, plus a special jet stove which could be used in any weather and would avoid the need to eat out all the time. The whole lot weighed less than the old mattress did on its own, so I was all set to take off again any time the notion took me. But first I needed to get caught up with everything at home.

I had cycled 818 miles, camped, stayed with friends new and old, slept in the caravan and in Bed and Breakfast establishments. I had done twenty-one workshops, including the impromptu one in the caravan, dropped in to the Cycle Audax in Dingwall and drummed with a Samba band. What a wonderful, wonderful adventure!

Fig. 141: Janet gets home

a bit more about the Knit 1 Bike 1 art work

The crocheted art work from the project now forms an exhibition, chronicling the journey. It includes all the things mentioned in the book and many more, and will tour small galleries and other venues in Scotland. Check my website for details of forthcoming exhibitions and associated workshops - www.createwithfibre.co.uk

Here is some more of the work created before, during and after the journey. My local knitting group helped to make things and various groups encountered on the way contributed pieces to the exhibition too.

Fig. 142: a packet of smoked salmon found at the side of the road

Finding a packet of smoked salmon at the side of the road made me wonder about its story. Had someone thrown it out of a passing car in the midst of an argument? Had a dog run off with it? I objected to the waste and decided to crochet it, using cotton yarn and double crochet for the packet. The salmon was done using finer yarn and slip stitch, taking ages to do. The sheep's skull in the centre of the piece below was found on a beach. I crocheted around it and added horns using handspun Blue Faced Leicester wool, and silk, then stuffed and then stiffened them.

Fig. 143: sheep's head with brown eyes

Caterpillars like the one in fig. 144 tended to crawl across the road and needed rescuing. Given my tendency to rescue all sorts of creepy crawlies I just had to make one.

The dandelions, bluebells and harebells in fig. 147 were crocheted or knitted, depending on the preference of those making them. These were part of a community project, started by my local knitting group Dalmellington Knit 'n' Blether, who wanted to help with the project. Their help was very much appreciated and it sparked off the idea of collecting contributions from other knitting groups I visited on the way.

Fig. 144: crocheted caterpillar

Fig. 145: spiders are favourite because they're fellow spinners

The dandelion seed heads were made from small pom poms using Rowan Kidsilk Haze. The stems for all of the above were made in knitted I-cord using two double-pointed needles and knitted around pipe cleaners.

Fig. 146: Glenfinnan Viaduct, Feb 2016

knitted bluebells, harebells, & dandelions – patterns

key for all patterns

St = Stitch, yo = yarn over needle, k = knit, K2tog = knit 2 together, d/k = double knitting yarn, ch = chain

harebells

materials - flower

3mm needles –ideally short ones. D/K yarn small quantity in each of lilac/pale blue/pale pink. Doing flowers in a mixture of these colours works well but just using a single colour is fine too. Keep the colours the same on any one stem.

materials – stem

Two 3mm double pointed needles ideally short ones. Dark or mid green D/K yarn. Two long pipe cleaners ideally green or dark coloured.

Fig. 147: crocheted and knitted dandelions and bluebells, some of which were created by Dalmellington Knit n' Blether group

flower – make several

Do not worry too much about exact stitch numbers - if you end up with an extra stitch here and there just knit it. I quite often forget which row I am on and just ad lib. It will work anyway.

Cast on 20 sts.

Row 1 Knit

Row 2 purl

Row 3 (K4 yo K2tog) repeat to end to make picot edge. Knit any odd sts

Row 4 Purl

Row 5 (K3 K2Tog) repeat to end. K1 if spare stitch at end

Row 6 purl

Row 7 knit

Row 8 purl

Row 9 (k3 k2tog) repeat to end. Knit any spare stitches

Row 10 purl

Row 11 K2 tog to end of row

Draw yarn through remaining sts. Sew up side. Fold cast on edge and sew up so that picots show.

stem - made with 'I' cord knitted around pipe cleaners

Twist the pipe cleaners firmly together and set aside.

Using the 2 double pointed needles size 3mm and D/K yarn in green, cast on 3 sts. Do not turn needles. Instead, slide sts to other end of needle. Pull yarn across the back of the knitting and knit in same direction again. Slide sts to other end and repeat. You are knitting in the round because of stranding the yarn across the back.

After two rows, insert the tip of the pipe cleaners into the hole in the centre of the knitting. Continue to work as above, ensuring that the yarn now goes around the pipe cleaners when it is stranded across the back. Continue to knit until the pipe cleaners are covered with knitting, working your way up them as you knit. It will be a bit awkward at first but it soon gets easier.

Cast off. Roll the stem vigorously between your hands to even the knitting out.

NB: an alternative is to simply wrap yarn around the pipe cleaners to make a stem, if you struggle with the I-cord.

making up

Sew 3-4 flowers to the top half of the stem, spacing them out. Use green yarn and leave a short length of yarn between each flower and the main stem when sewing them on. The flowers will thus each have a mini stem of their own where they are attached to the main stem.

bluebells

Knit as for Canterbury bells but with two rows in between decrease rows and miss out picot edge. Add 6-12 flowers per stem, clustered around top half of stem.

crocheted dandelions

Using D/K yellow yarn and 3mm hook, ch 6.

Miss 1 chain and slip st back along remaining 5 Ch.

Ch 6 again and repeat.

Repeat above for desired number of petals on outer layer.

Ch 5. Miss 1 ch and slip st back along remaining 4 sts. Repeat for number of petals desired for middle layer.

Ch 4. Miss 1 ch and slip st back along remaining 3 sts. Repeat for number of petals desired for centre of flower.

Coil round in layers and stitch together.

stem

Knit I cord round pipe cleaner as described for bluebells, but using one small pipe-cleaner. Alternatively wrap yarn around pipe cleaner.

knitted dandelions

Row 1 Cast on 9 sts.

Row 2 cast off till 1 st remains, knitting into back of loop.

Repeat above 2 rows 8 times in total.

Continue as below:

Row 1 cast on 8 sts

Row 2 cast off till 1 st remains, knitting into back of loop.

Repeat 6 times in total.

Continue as below:

Row 1 cast on 7 sts

Row 2 cast off till 1 st remains, knitting into back of loop.

Repeat 4 times in total.

Coil so that petals sit in layers and sew together, with largest petals underneath and shorter ones on top. Work stem as for crocheted dandelions.

other lowimpact.org titles

See lowimpact.org/about/lowimpact-org-publications

 **The loveliest Loo:** tells of a girl's unexpected discovery of a different kind of toilet, a compost toilet... and one with a surprise! *The Loveliest Loo* will make you laugh as you ponder the most basic elements of life and how we regard them. A charming story about a beautifully simple way to conserve our natural resources. The striking black and white images are designed to be coloured using pencils.

Timber for Building: from growing and felling trees, to selecting the right wood for the tasks you have in mind, this book explains how to efficiently convert low value local round wood to high value sawn material and get the best out of your equipment, before outlining different drying methods and taking you on to preparing the timber for your project.

 **Food Smoking:** in our cave-dwelling days, food smoking was used to preserve food and then our ancestors discovered just how great it makes food taste. This book covers the basics of cold and hot smoking; delves into the principles of combustion and explains brining and dry salt curing, plus how to source wood for smoking and provides plans for building a cold smoker and smoke generators.

How to Build a Wind Pump: the wind pump described in this book can pump rainwater, greywater, river, pond or well water for irrigation, aerate a fish pond, run a water feature or even be a bird scarer. The turbine is 700mm diameter, and the head plus rotor weighs less than 4kg. In a light-to-moderate wind, it should pump 1000 litres per day, with a head of 3-5 metres.

Herbal Remedies: teaches you to identify, grow and harvest medicinal plants. It shows you how to make a range of simple medicines including ointments, salves, syrups, oils, compresses, infusions and decoctions. There are sections on body systems, explaining which herbs are useful for a range of ailments, and detailed herb monographs. This second edition has been revised to take account of recent changes in UK legislation.

Make your own essential oils: a fascinating hobby, or for the professional aromatherapist, a way of ensuring that your products are fresh, unadulterated and organic. This book also describes how to make creams, lotions, balms, gels, tinctures and other skin-care products from the essential oils and distillate waters you have produced.

Wind & Solar Electricity: there are chapters on the various system components required, how to put them all together, batteries, grid-connected systems, and there is even a basic electricity primer. Andy has analysed the output of his system for over 10 years, and these real-life figures are included. Developments in the associated technology and UK government incentives have led him to make substantial revisions and additions for this second edition.

Make Your Own Natural Soaps includes both hot and cold process soap making, with step-by-step instructions. There are extensive bar, liquid and cream soap recipes, full details of the equipment needed to make a start and a re-batching chapter just in case anything goes wrong! And for anyone interested in turning their new skills to profit there is information on the legislation and regulations you need to comply with to be able to sell soap.

Heating with Wood: covers everything you need to know about wood heating, from planning a system, choosing, sizing, installing & making a stove, obtaining & storing firewood and cooking with wood, to heating your water with a back boiler. It includes chainsaw use, basic forestry, health & safety, chimneys, pellet and woodchip stoves and how to light a fire and keep it going.

Compost Toilets : reduce water usage, prevent pollution and produce fertiliser. Built properly they can be attractive, family friendly and low maintenance. Contains everything you need to know about building a compost toilet, plus proprietary models, decomposition, pathogens and hygiene, use and maintenance, environmental benefits and troubleshooting.

Solar Hot Water: particularly applicable to domestic dwellings in the UK, although the principles described are widely adopted throughout the developed world. This book provides a comprehensive introduction to every aspect of solar hot water, including relevant equipment, components, system design and installation and even how to build your own panels.

How to Spin: a veritable encyclopedia of spinning know-how. Comprehensive instructions allow new spinners to get started with the minimum of equipment and give those who have a wheel already a full understanding of its operation. The chapter on 'other fibres' offers a wealth of information about fibres as diverse as yak and SeaCell, as well as information on the preparation and spinning of silk

notes